ACTIVE LEARNING

Handbook

for the

MULTIPLE INTELLIGENCES CLASSROOM

James Bellanca

SkyLight
TRAINING AND PUBLISHING, INC.
Arlington Heights, Illinois

Active Learning Handbook for the Multiple Intelligences Classroom

Published by IRI/SkyLight Training and Publishing, Inc.
2626 S. Clearbook Dr., Arlington Heights, IL 60005
800-348-4474 or 847-290-6600
Fax 847-290-6609
info@iriskylight.com
http://www.iriskylight.com

Creative Director: Robin Fogarty
Managing Editor: Barbara Harold
Editors: Barb Lightner, Monica Phillips
Graphic Designer: Bruce Leckie
Cover and Illustration Designer: David Stockman
Production Supervisor: Bob Crump
Type Compositor: Donna Ramirez

ISBN 1-57517-071-X
LCCCN 97-70718

1826C-7-98McN
Item number 1466

06 05 04 03 02 01 00 99 98   15 14 13 12 11 10 9 8 7 6 5 4 3

*To all teachers who are striving
to make learning an active, rewarding
experience for their students.*

ACKNOWLEDGMENTS

I offer my deepest appreciation to the many mentors and collaborators who made the content of this book possible. From Peggy Pink, my department chairperson at New Trier High School, who encouraged me as a young teacher to attend my first active participation workshop, to my current SkyLight colleagues, Robin Fogarty and Kay Burke, who invent new practices at a frenetic pace, my life thoughts and teaching have been enriched by an endless number of master teachers. These include Merrill Harman, Howie Kirschenbaum, and Sidney Simon, who conducted that first workshop. Through Howie and the Sagamore Institute, I add Joel Goodman and Margie Ingram, Eliott Masie, Rod Napier, Roger Johnson, David Johnson, and Jack Canfield. Through Roger and David, I can chart what I learned from Bob Slavin, Elizabeth Cohen, Richard Schmuck, and the Sharans. Searching for answers to questions about cooperative learning led me to Art Costa, John Barell, and others who focused me on the active engagement of the mind.

Beyond the classroom, I owe Larry Chase, Marie Meyers, Phil Harris, Mary Kay Kickles, Bill Peters, and a long, long list of classroom teachers for encouraging the application of active learning practices to our teacher training programs. Foremost among the teachers were my inspired and inspiring colleagues at New Trier's Center for Self-Directed Learning—Arlene Paul, Bob Applebaum, Vernoy Johnson, and Bill Gregory—who demonstrated and proved "way back when" the power and the benefit of classrooms where students were the core of active engagement in authentic learning experiences.

To each and every one, I say, "thank you."

CONTENTS

SECTION ONE
Verbal/Linguistic

SECTION TWO

Logical/Mathematical

SECTION THREE

Visual/Spatial

SECTION FOUR

Bodily/Kinesthetic

SECTION FIVE

Musical/Rhythmic

SECTION SIX

Interpersonal

SECTION SEVEN

Intrapersonal

SECTION EIGHT

Naturalist

IRI/SkyLight Training and Publishing, Inc.

INTRODUCTION

Mr. Rimston frowned. "Pamela, I don't understand," he said. "You spent the entire period making this sketch of me talking to the class. You didn't take a single note. What were you thinking?"

Pamela shrugged, "I don't know. When you're talking to us it's like I don't hear a word."

"You didn't hear a word I said?" asked the teacher.

"No, but what I saw made a lot of sense to me."

All the time Tim Rimston was delivering his well-organized lecture of the principles of culture, Pamela had paid close attention, but she didn't hear a word he said. Instead, her fingers squeezed her thick lead pencil and sketched the details of her teacher's face. Over and over, she caught his many expressions from different angles until she had a collage of heads. Now, it was difficult for him to comprehend what was going on in the head of this articulate student who drew so well.

This is one example of an intelligence clash. A lecturing teacher is an example of an individual with a strong verbal/linguistic intelligence. As learning psychologist Howard Gardner (1983) has characterized, individuals with this intelligence, the type that dominates curriculum and instruction in most schools, are bound to be successful when the ability to use the written and spoken word is dominant. A daydreaming, doodling student, on the other hand, has a dominant visual/spatial intelligence. That student doesn't focus on words. He or she focuses on the images, processes the pictures, and ends the class period not with notes but with sketches.

This clash of intelligences may seem extreme. But, following Gardner's theory to its logical conclusion, it is easier to understand why the way many students learn and understand doesn't seem to fit the dominant intelligences implicit in most teaching that happens in classrooms. Students in contemporary classrooms are most likely to be taught by teachers who have a well-developed verbal/linguistic (words) or logical/mathematical (numbers) intelligence. If a student's intelligence aligns with one or both of these, that student has a better chance of understanding the assigned schoolwork, earning higher grades, and testing well on the standardized tests that measure in terms of those two intelligences. On the other hand, if the student is strong in one of the other intelligences identified by Gardner, that student may not do as well in the school setting as his or her counterpart who identifies with the verbal/linguistic or logical/mathematical intelligence.

GARDNER'S MULTIPLE INTELLIGENCES

Verbal/linguistic intelligence is the intelligence of words, or the ability to use the core operations of language with clarity. By communicating through reading, writing, listening, or speaking, the significant components of this intelligence are employed. More important, the use of this intelligence helps link prior knowledge and understanding to new information and explains how the linkage occurs. The verbal/ linguistic intelligence enables personal perceptions to be communicated and is highly valued in schools.

Verbal/linguistic intelligence helps students produce and refine language use in many formats. The ability to form and recognize words and their patterns by sight, sound, and, for some, touch is a start. The techniques of language, such as metaphor, hyperbole, symbol, and grammar, are next. These are enriched with meaning by abstract reasoning, conceptual patterns, feeling, tone, structure, and an expanding vocabulary across the curriculum. Ultimately, the peaks of language development are reached by those who combine sound and sense in unique patterns to express themselves.

The value of the verbal/linguistic intelligence is emphasized through testing reading and language arts and comprehension in other content areas. How well a student performs in mathematics, for instance, is interwoven with his or her ability to comprehend the test questions.

Logical/mathematical intelligence is the intelligence of numbers and reasoning, or the ability to use inductive and deductive reasoning, solve abstract problems, and understand the complex relationships of interrelated concepts, ideas, and things.

This intelligence includes the skills of classifying, predicting, prioritizing, formulating scientific hypotheses, and understanding cause-effect relationships. Reasoning skills apply to a broad array of areas and include using logical thinking in science, social studies, literature, and other areas such as word processing, creating and reading spreadsheets, learning a foreign language, building a model, using the Internet, and learning a sequence of musical notation.

Young children develop this intelligence as they work with concrete manipulatives and grasp the concept of one-to-one relationships and numeration. They advance from concrete to representational ideas in the form of symbolic language, working equations, and formulas they learn about abstraction through the world of logic. The critical thinking skills of sequencing, analyzing, and estimating are taught in most school curricula, but need to be emphasized through active learning activities.

Visual/spatial intelligence is the intelligence of pictures and images, or the capacity to perceive the visual world accurately and be able to recreate one's visual experiences. It involves the ability to see form, color, shape, and texture in the "mind's eye" and to transfer these to concrete representation in art forms.

This intelligence begins with the sharpening of sensorimotor perceptions. The eye discriminates color, shape, form, texture, spatial depth, dimension, and relationships. As the intelligence develops, hand-eye coordination and small-muscle control enable the individual to reproduce the perceived shapes and colors in a variety of media. The painter, sculptor, architect, gardener, cartographer, drafter, and graphic designer all transfer images in their minds to the new object they are creating or improving. In this way, visual perceptions are mixed with prior knowledge, experience, emotions, and images to create a new vision for others to experience.

Bodily/kinesthetic intelligence is the intelligence of the whole body and the hands. This intelligence enables us to control and interpret body motions, manipulate physical objects, and establish harmony between the mind and the body. The Spartans of ancient Greece built their culture around the importance of the body, its looks, and its performance. In modern times, the Olympic Games carry on this tradition.

It is a mistake, however, to think that the development of this intelligence is limited to athletics. A surgeon's fine small-motor control when performing an intricate heart operation or an airplane navigator's ability to fine-tune the instruments also are developments of this intelligence.

Musical/rhythmic intelligence is the intelligence of tone, rhythm, and timbre and starts with the degree of sensitivity one has to a pattern of sounds and the ability to respond emotionally. As students develop their musical awareness, they develop the fundamentals of this intelligence.

This intelligence grows as students increase their sophistication when listening to and hearing music. It further develops as students create more complex and subtle variations of musical patterns, develop talent on musical instruments, and advance to complex compositions.

Interpersonal intelligence is the intelligence of social understanding, or the ability to understand and relate to others. Those exhibiting this intelligence notice and distinguish moods, temperaments, motivations, and intentions. For example, at a simple level, this intelligence is seen in children who notice and are sensitive to the moods of the adults around them. A more complex interpersonal skill is an adult's ability to read and interpret the hidden intentions of others.

This intelligence includes the capacity to understand and interact with other people with a win-win result. Interpersonal intelligence involves verbal and nonverbal communication skills, collaborative skills, conflict management, consensus-building skills, and the ability to trust, respect, lead, and motivate others to the achievement of a mutually beneficial goal. Empathy for feelings, fears, anticipations, and beliefs of others, the willingness to listen without judgment, and the desire to help others raise their level of performance to its highest are all critical traits of those with a strong interpersonal intelligence.

Intrapersonal intelligence is the intelligence of self-knowledge, or the ability to know oneself and assume responsibility for one's life and learning. The individual with a strong intrapersonal intelligence is able to understand his or her range of emotions and draw on them to direct his or her behavior. This individual thrives on time to think, to reflect, and to complete self-assessments. The need for such introspection makes this intelligence the most private. In Gardner's words, "the intrapersonal intelligence amounts to little more than the capacity to

                                                      IRI/SkyLight Training and Publishing, Inc.

distinguish a feeling of pleasure from one of pain and, on the basis of such discrimination, to become more involved in or to withdraw from a situation" (1983, 239).

This intelligence enables learners to take greater responsibility for their lives and learning. Too few students, Gardner suggests, realize they can take responsibility for their learning, especially when they attend schools that base recognition of achievements on external motivations.

The naturalist intelligence, which Gardner added to his original seven in 1995, is the intelligence of nature and springs from an individual's ability to recognize species of plants and animals in the environment and to create taxonomies that classify the many different subspecies. Individuals such as Charles Darwin, John Audubon, Louis Agassiz, and E. O. Wilson are well-known naturalists. Young children who can pick out different types of flowers, name different types of animals, or even arrange such items as shoes, cars, or designer clothes into common categories are budding naturalists.

The connection to naturalistic learning is obvious in botany and zoology, while individuals who work in organic chemistry, entomology, medicine, photography, civil engineering, and a host of other fields also must develop their naturalist skills.

MINIMALIST APPROACH

In the past decade, the conflict between teachers' and schools' dominant intelligences and the strongest intelligences of many students has become more evident. As a result, the visual and musical arts, sciences, and other curricula that traditionally encouraged students to learn in their own ways are being threatened. Schools are responding to declining funding and increasing student populations by taking a "minimalist approach," demanding programs that teach students with the fastest reading and arithmetic results and the least fuss.

What is this minimalist approach? In the past several decades, textbook publishers, influenced by social forces, have perfected product lines that align curriculum, instruction, and assessment while attaining minimal content standards. The publishers, some owned by conglomerates that also own the test-making companies, have led the way in making it easy for schools and teachers to show results by the measurement of skills and competencies. What is measurable? So far, the testing companies can measure only bits and pieces of information because they have yet to find a valid or reliable way to measure how well students understand information or how well they transfer what they have learned. As a result of the importance placed on measurable standards, "teacher-proof" classrooms have been created that require teachers to follow a strict curriculum and allow little flexibility to be creative or tailor teaching style to the needs of the students.

Among those who oppose the minimalist approach are Richard Murnane, a Harvard economist, and Frank Levy, an MIT economist, who together wrote *Teaching the New Basic Skills: Principles for Educating Children to Thrive in a Changing Economy* (1996). They argue that despite a changing economic structure, schools have retained a nineteenth-century minimalist curriculum. Murnane and Levy show the mismatch between the knowledge and skills needed to survive in a modern, high-performing workplace and those that are being taught in today's schools.

Murnane and Levy do not deny the need for mathematics and literacy. They do question the low level of these skills that are expected as well as the nonemphasis given to working in teams (interpersonal intelligence), solving problems (intrapersonal intelligence), and the ability to organize information (logical/mathematical intelligence).

BEYOND LEARNING FOR RECALL

Other voices add hard facts that support the idea that teaching and learning are more than just the recall of facts and figures. Among these are Anne Brown and Anne Palincsar (1989), who have shown the powerful effects of metacognition. Their work with reciprocal teaching, a key active learning strategy, illustrated what can happen when teachers have the opportunity to focus students' attention on the process of reading using the process of prediction.

Israeli cognitive psychologist Reuven Feuerstein also adds his beliefs. Feuerstein (1985) has demonstrated how challenging cognitive approaches can lead to radical changes in learning performance, even by students labeled "unteachable." The success of his program, Instrumental Enrichment, which changes cognitive performance, depends on

IRI/SkyLight Training and Publishing, Inc.

a process called mediation. This process requires a teacher who is prepared to help children discover their capacity to solve complex problems. Research studies show improved learning performance when teachers as mediators help students learn how to be active generators of knowledge rather than passive receptors of factual information.

Gardner, Feuerstein, Brown, and Palincsar are but a few who have demonstrated through research the benefits of learning in ways that challenge students to go beyond what is measurable. When challenging students, they argue, educators need to realize that there are many more ways to teach than by rote alone. There is teaching for understanding, decision making, problem solving, and connecting a part to a whole, detail to concept, and concept to concept. There also is inference, prediction, analysis for bias, and learning for transfer. Each of these processes requires some form of critical thinking. All are processes that students can develop and refine.

To garner understanding, students need to learn to gather and process information with precision and accuracy from multiple sources. Unlike bygone days when information was selected and passed along through a teacher's lecture or a textbook, information in a high-tech world comes from a plethora of sources, of which only two are the teacher and the textbook. Television, the World Wide Web, CD-ROMs, and other tools place students in the role of selective information gatherers. In order to choose wisely from a variety of sources, students who learn to analyze data for bias, make correct inferences, classify, and synthesize are better prepared to understand and use information from a multitude of sources.

How well a student understands and processes data can determine how well he or she performs in a variety of school tasks and how well prepared he or she is for the real world of work tasks. In the classroom, how a student deciphers the meaning of classic literature or a science project can prepare him or her to use these understandings and insights in life. It also better prepares him or her to more easily pass through the SAT/ACT test gates. How well a student applies problem-solving processes to algebra or geometry helps when he or she takes trigonometry and calculus. Younger students who learn only computation or how to memorize facts may test well, but they will have much less chance to develop the necessary skills for lifelong learning.

TRANSFER-ORIENTED CURRICULUM

Any curriculum designed to promote students as critical thinkers must allow time for teachers to work on the development of the thinking processes. This works best when the teaching of critical thinking is the foundation upon which other teaching builds. In order for the content curriculum to develop students' understanding, teachers need to develop students' cognitive skills that are implicit in the content. For example, in the fourth grade reading curriculum, the teacher will have to teach students how to draw inferences and make predictions. In the ninth grade writing curriculum, the teacher needs to teach students how to connect specific arguments to general statements and apply those across many content areas.

Using a critical-thinking approach to curriculum challenges teachers to develop instructional techniques that will help students prepare for the world beyond the school walls. Critical-thinking approaches develop students' abilities to understand and transfer what they are learning to real-life situations. As David Perkins (1988) pointed out, teaching for transfer doesn't just happen; skilled teachers "shepherd" the transfer across the curriculum and beyond the school walls. In a *transfer-oriented instruction* mode, a critical-thinking curriculum opens the door to authentic assessments that can tell teachers what students know and what students can do. Authentic assessment techniques such as observation checklists and video demonstrations go well beyond short-answer tests. These tools not only tell what factual information the student recalls, but also show how well the student can use knowledge and skills in novel situations. In a *fact-based classroom*, students may match chemical symbols with the proper element name, while in a transfer-based classroom a teacher can check how well the student uses his or her knowledge of chemical elements to complete an experiment. By combining elements from both fact-based and transfer-oriented strategies, a language arts teacher can not only give a fill-in-the-blank quiz to check what punctuation the sixth grade students can identify, he or she also can set criteria for the use of punctuation in an essay and look to see that students can use the punctuation rules in their essays.

Opportunities for students to develop critical thinking processes are not found in classrooms dominated by the regurgitation of short answers. They are found in classrooms where active learning is an essential component.

 IRI/SkyLight Training and Publishing, Inc.

ACTIVE LEARNING

Active learning operates at many levels in a challenging classroom. On one level, active learning gives students a chance to do something that produces an immediate effect several times during a class or the school day. The teacher may plan a sequence of tasks that require physical movements or check for students' understanding by a thumbs up signal system. The teacher may select basic bodily/kinesthetic strategies such as the *carousel, human graph,* or *four corners* (see glossary) and require students to move around or have individuals do boardwork, make a presentation, or demonstrate a skill.

At a more complex level, the active learning teacher constructs learning tasks that require students to work "hands on." First grade students may discover patterns by building simple houses with colored blocks. Intermediate students may study buoyancy by floating pumpkins, oranges, and pine nuts in a sink. Eighth graders may investigate the justice system by having a trial, and high school geometry students may study radius and circumference with tape measures and paper plates of many sizes or use their visual/spatial intelligence to study the use of triangles in a modern skyscraper.

At the highest level, active learning uses the active engagement of the students' thinking processes in learning and applying knowledge. There are five criteria that mark this engagement of students as mindful learners: focus activity, cooperative structure, mediation, transfer, and evaluation.

Focus Activity

In large group instruction, the teacher may engage all students in gathering information through several intelligence-based strategies. These strategies *focus* reluctant learners on the lesson. There are many observable strategies and student responses that can be indicators of this criterion. For example, the teacher may use *wraparounds, three-level questions, think-pair-shares,* or *random checks* (see glossary) to prompt student responses or provide a format for responding. The best activities are based on the intelligence needs of the students in each given class.

Cooperative Structure

In small group instruction, the teacher engages all students in a *collaborative*, hands-on *task* related to a single curricular goal. The teacher assigns group roles, monitors participation, checks for understanding, assesses contributions and knowledge gained, and may post *performance rubrics*. Students learn content by working in a cooperative interpersonal structure, performing assigned roles, assisting others in learning, and sharing responsibility for a group task.

Mediation

The teacher *mediates* each student's achievement of curricular goals. For example, the teacher challenges students to change, individuates instruction, promotes sharing behavior, seeks student responses, and encourages self-regulation of behavior. Students respond to questions and visual goals, control their own behavior, make connections among ideas, explain why when responding to questions, and develop their intrapersonal intelligence.

Transfer

The teacher shows students how to understand the lesson and how to *transfer* content. The teacher identifies implicit thinking processes, labels and demonstrates the thinking, structures tasks requiring thinking processes, and teaches strategies that facilitate process use. Students describe and plan thinking processes and monitor and assess their own thinking processes. Very often, the teacher may rely on graphic organizers that stimulate the visual/spatial intelligence.

Evaluation

The teacher *evaluates* student learning by using a variety of assessment approaches. These approaches include teacher-made tests that gauge recall, understanding, and application; rubrics for performance, products, and projects; student self-assessments and reflections; and a variety of evidences, such as written and oral responses and videos. Students perform self-assessments, keep portfolios of their best work, and reflect on standards of performance through journal writing and other guided activities that stimulate a variety of intelligences.

By using Gardner's theory of multiple intelligences, a teacher can highlight ways to structure an active learning environment. On one

IRI/SkyLight Training and Publishing, Inc.

level, Gardner's theory helps a teacher select active instructional methods congruent to the class's varied intelligences. For students who learn best by seeing and touching, the teacher can include active learning strategies and materials that challenge their visual/spatial and bodily/kinesthetic intelligences. For students who learn better through reflection, the curriculum can include paired think-alouds (see glossary) and journal responses that spark the intrapersonal intelligence.

Since most curricula are tailored to the verbal/linguistic and logical/mathematical intelligences, it is especially important for the teacher to engage the many students who learn better through the other six intelligences by including a variety of intelligence-appropriate strategies. By using active strategies that awaken and engage all eight intelligences, the teacher gives all students a more equitable chance to learn even the most challenging material and to remember it.

By designing active strategies that engage each student's strongest learning skills, a teacher evens out the learning field. An equal learning field provides each student, regardless of wealth, race, natural origin, sex, or past success pattern in school, with a better chance to succeed academically. By using a variety of strategies representative of all the intelligences, the teacher can make great strides toward the goal of "equity," and provide each student with a fairer opportunity to learn.

THE CHALLENGE PRINCIPLE

Reuven Feuerstein (1985), an Israeli cognitive psychologist, has developed systems for mediating children that others have labeled "impossible to teach." These systems have proven successful in cultures around the world. He identifies "challenge" as a core responsibility of the effective user of active learning strategies.

Consider students in two different elementary classrooms. In one, the teacher hands out a worksheet with 50 fill-in-the-blank questions about a story they just read. The students are instructed how to fill in the blanks as the teacher monitors their work. One half hour later, students are told to pass their worksheets forward. The worksheets are set aside for the teacher to grade at home. In the next half hour, students may complete true and false statements on another worksheet or do similar pencil-and-paper tasks. The pattern continues throughout the school day.

In another classroom, the teacher divides the class into mixed-ability groups of three, giving each group three short stories. The teacher then reviews the goals for the reading lesson, presents a *rubric* showing expectations, and invites the students in each group to share how they will help each other reach those goals. As the students work, the teacher walks among the groups to coach, provide information, and note progress. After a designated time period, the teacher guides the students through a review of what they learned and the problem-solving skills they used to compare the three stories. After the review, the students are given feedback on what they did well and prepare for the next, more difficult reading task.

When a teacher follows a successful learning experience with a more difficult task in the same vein, he or she mediates "challenge." This experience is similar to that of an advanced skater when he or she masters a difficult jump or spin and then moves to the next level of difficulty. Doing a single axel well is good, but it is not enough to keep the skater's interest. The skater needs to move on to the double, the triple, and, eventually, combinations.

What are the specific responsibilities of the teacher who understands the motivational value of challenge in the active learning classroom? First, the teacher presents an *open and excited attitude* about taking on a challenge. When students show concern, the teacher acknowledges the difficulty of the challenge, empathizes, and provides support and encouragement. "Remember," the teacher says, "how you did on the last tough assignment. Together, we can do this one."

Second, the teacher prepares a *sequence* of increasingly *complex tasks* and charts the pathway to success. Instead of boring, repetitive worksheets that just "get done," the teacher provides active learning opportunities that are increasingly difficult.

Third, the teacher structures tasks that *require taking risks* to complete. He or she helps students consider a variety of ways to overcome doubts and fears and finish the task.

Finally, the teacher *teaches strategies* that students can use to handle their personal difficult challenges in a self-directed way. To do this, the teacher builds in the time for students to apply new problem-solving strategies to an increasingly difficult curriculum. In the challenge classroom, there is no regression.

The multiple intelligences prism allows teachers to design lessons that follow the challenge principle. In addition to allowing the teacher to teach students established and strong ways of learning, the teacher can design ways to introduce and improve other ways of learning. Thus, in any lesson, unit, or project, the teacher can integrate several intelligences. This is so even when the curriculum, such as mathematics, forces a primary focus on a specific intelligence.

Consider the following example. In the fourth grade, fractions are an important unit. In a typical workbook, the logical/mathematical approach stands alone. In order to challenge students who find mathematics boring or difficult, the teacher can integrate other intelligences into the instruction of fractions. First, the teacher can present a pie or cake and have students cut it into two, four, and eight parts (bodily/kinesthetic). She or he can pair students (interpersonal) and assign the pairs to cut pictures of houses or offices into equal parts (bodily/kinesthetic), to divide clothespins or toothpicks into equal piles (bodily/kinesthetic), or to draw trees with a set number in each group (visual/spatial). In addition, the teacher can ask students to write a letter explaining why fractions are important (verbal/linguistic) or sing a verse about the importance of fractions (musical/rhythmic).

ACTIVE LEARNING AND TIME

A common concern expressed about active learning lessons is "it takes more time." This is true. Active learning lessons can take more time to plan, gather materials, complete, and assess. If, however, the teacher designs the lesson or unit for student understanding and transfer abilities as the final objectives, the results in terms of achievement (as measured by teacher-made and standardized test scores) by students in their understanding and ability to transfer (as measured by diverse performance assessments) will more than compensate for the increased time and effort.

In actuality, the time issue may concern only the novice user of active learning strategies. As the teacher-designer moves toward expert status, he or she is most likely to find the following: (1) in-class time or multidimensional lessons and projects take less time than was previously spent in one-dimensional classroom work; (2) preparation time for each use of a well-designed unit eventually becomes reduced to refinements that increase student engagement and learning results; (3) assessment requires less and less after-class grading time as students' observable in-class performance provides more valid and reliable data; and (4) increased student engagement propelled by students' growing intrinsic motivation to learn leads to other useful active learning strategies.

ABOUT THE BOOK

The first title in IRI/SkyLight's line of Shoebox Curriculum™ books, *Active Learning Handbook* contains 200 practical, "ready-to-wear" active learning strategies that can be implemented immediately in the K–12 classroom. Three criteria were used to select each strategy:

- ❑ A research base indicates its effectiveness for increasing achievement.
- ❑ Support from practicing classroom teachers who have used the strategy with success.
- ❑ Strategy used by the author/educator with students successfully or observed by the author/educator as a successful strategy with students.

Active learning activities are organized by the eight intelligences. Do note, however, that many activities lend themselves to more than one intelligence. Each activity lists the purpose, when to use, the necessary materials, and how to do the activity. Variations of each activity provide ways to adapt a strategy to different content areas or to integrate multiple intelligences.

Blackline masters are provided in a separate section for specific handouts referenced in activities. As many of these handouts are used in a variety of activities, they are organized alphabetically by their titles rather than in relation to the chapter in which they appear.

Note the glossary and bibliography for further clarification of concepts and strategies and additional readings.

HOW TO USE THE BOOK

Active learning strategies are often fun. It is easy to use many of these strategies as "filler" activities. On Friday afternoon, a teacher may pick a fun strategy to fill any empty time. Using active learning strategies as an occasional filler is appropriate when a teacher wants to lighten the moment or provide a welcome release from the day's stress.

However, filler time activities alone fail to take advantage of the potential of active learning strategies. An active learning strategy is an activity used with a specific learning purpose. It is best to select a strategy so that students have a better chance of attaining a lesson's goals. When designing lessons and units teachers should incorporate the following active learning strategies:

❏ *Differentiate* the most important concepts students need to learn through the lesson or unit.

❏ *Identify* the most appropriate large group, small group, and individual instructional strategies that will enable all students to accomplish the lesson goals.

❏ *Establish challenging performance standards* for both lesson content and the learning process.

❏ *Identify what mediated learning interactions* are necessary to ensure high achievement of each student.

❏ *Use an instructional design* that ensures the *incorporation* of the *most* appropriate active learning strategies. Such a strong design will:

• Start the lesson, unit, or goal with a knowledge check or provide some sort of knowledge.

• Make clear the performance expectations.

• Provide adequate information resources.

• Provide clear instructions for each task.

• Incorporate a variety of strategies individuated to multiple ways of learning.

• Bridge learning between tasks.

• Mediate individual achievement.

• Provide for multiple forms of assessment.

• Maintain a balanced pace.

The design of active learning strategies is a challenge well within the reach of all teachers. It is in the grasp of those who see clearly the opportunity to raise student achievement by raising the level of their own teaching performance. With the goal of teaching mindful learners who actively pursue knowledge, the teachers do become active learners.

IRI/SkyLight Training and Publishing, Inc.

SECTION ONE

VERBAL/ LINGUISTIC

VOCABULARY BANK

ACTIVITY-AT-A-GLANCE

Purpose

Connect new concepts with prior knowledge by maintaining a vocabulary bank.

When to Use

Use in sequenced lessons or a unit of study where previous vocabulary forms a foundation for the next lesson.

What You'll Need

❏ Journals or notebooks

What to Do

1. On the overhead or board, post 4–7 key vocabulary words that students learned in previous units. Review their definitions and discuss their importance in the upcoming lesson or unit.

2. Invite students to start a vocabulary section in their journals or notebooks. After reviewing the first set of words, identify 4–7 new key words and definitions to be studied in the lesson or unit.

3. Invite students to use their own words (and drawings if appropriate) to record meanings.

Variations

1. Use 3–5 words for primary students and 7–10 for secondary students.

2. After each set of new words is added, invite students to use a portmanteau strategy, the combining of 2 words to create another word with a new meaning, such as

    *   Toehole—a hole in one's sock that expands as one plays with it.
    *   Leaftover—the tiny piece of greenery stuck between someone's front teeth after eating a salad.

WHAT'S IT ALL ABOUT?

ACTIVITY-AT-A-GLANCE

Purpose

Preview and read textbook assignments, using predicting, scanning, and summarizing techniques.

When to Use

Use when preparing students to read new textbook assignments or articles.

What You'll Need

❏ Journals or notebooks

What to Do

1. Explain that students are going to learn some reading strategies or tricks that can help them study. Select a chapter from the textbook. Have students read the chapter's title, look at the pictures or diagrams, and predict what they will learn in the chapter. Write students' responses on the board or overhead.

2. Invite students to read the chapter's major headings. Ask how these headings give more insight into the chapter's content. Add the responses to the list on the board or overhead.

3. Have students read the information under the first major heading and compare it to their predictions. Ask if this information adds to, clarifies, contradicts, or simply repeats what they predicted. Add any new ideas to the list. Have students read the last section in the chapter and repeat the process of comparing the new information to their predictions.

IRI/SkyLight Training and Publishing, Inc.

Title – *The United States: The Early Years*

Predictions
1. It's about the Pilgrims
2. How we became a country
3. George Washington
4. The war we had with England
5. The people who started this country

4. Ask students to write brief summaries describing, confirming, or correcting their predictions. When they have finished, invite volunteers to read their summaries aloud. Discuss any missing information that should be added.

5. Assign pairs of students to read each of the chapter's remaining sections. After they have finished, ask for volunteers to compare their predictions with the actual information that they read. On the board or overhead, check off each prediction that is validated and end by reading or displaying samples of student summaries.

6. Review the process for previewing a text assignment and discuss the benefits of this approach:

   • Predict from title.
   • Scan the major subheadings (usually bold).
   • Predict after reviewing opening and closing paragraphs.

- Read each section and compare to predictions.
- Summarize the chapter.

Variations

1. Have students work in pairs throughout the process. Let pairs discuss the predictions before they share with the class.
2. Have each student keep his or her own list in a journal or notebook.
3. Follow up with an assignment using and documenting the process with the next chapter in the text.
4. Have students learn the process by using magazine articles.

Ideas

ISSUE EDITORIAL

ACTIVITY-AT-A-GLANCE

Purpose

Formulate and support a conclusion or point of view using factual information.

When to Use

Use when introducing a new lesson or new information.

What You'll Need

❏ Several copies of newspaper editorials

What to Do

1. Arrange students in pairs. Give each pair a copy of an editorial from the local newspaper. After students have read the editorial, help them list what information was used to argue the point of view.

2. Identify a key topic, issue, or concept from the next lesson or unit. Brainstorm with the class a list of what they know about the topic. Clarify all items on the list and assign 1 item to each pair of students. Instruct pairs to read the text and use additional resource materials to look for information that will expand or extend their basic knowledge.

3. When they have finished, instruct each pair to write an editorial that uses the research to support its point of view. After reviewing the editorials, invite pairs to read them aloud or display them on a bulletin board.

Variations

1. Divide class into 3–5 groups. Have each group organize as a newspaper or magazine team. Give each team a different set of resource materials on a topic. The team will then prepare a newsletter with an editorial and several short articles on the topic.

2. After brainstorming about a topic, create a class newspaper with editorials on subtopics, cartoons, ads, and news articles.

THE BIG PICTURE
A TEXTBOOK WALKTHROUGH

ACTIVITY-AT-A-GLANCE

Purpose

Gain an overview of course content by becoming familiar with the textbook.

When to Use

Use at the start of the semester for a class that will use a textbook on a regular basis.

What You'll Need

❏ Chart paper

What to Do

1. Invite students to walk through their textbooks and preview the entire course. Begin by posting 4–6 learning objectives for the course on the board or overhead and explaining them to the class.

2. Introduce students to the book's table of contents. Ask them to scan the chapter titles, index, and format of the chapters, including highlighted vocabulary, visuals, graphs and charts, questions, and references.

3. After this walkthrough, ask students to describe how the material is organized (e.g., sequentially, conceptually, by topic, etc.) and what highlights relate to the course's objectives.

4. Provide students with chart paper. If the text uses a sequential format, assign pairs of students to construct a timeline for the course using the chapter titles. If the text uses a topical or conceptual format, work

Concept Map

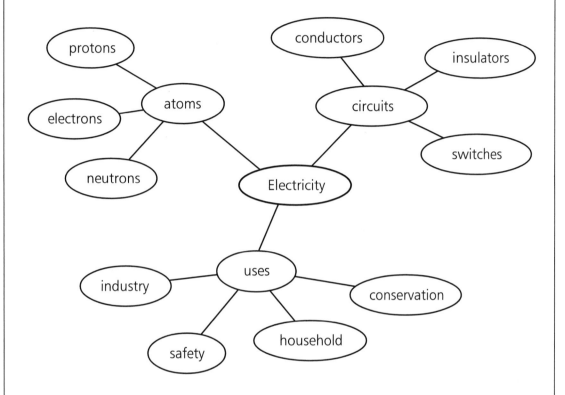

with students to construct a concept map for the course from the chapter titles. Post timelines or concept maps as a reference for use throughout the course.

Variations

1. Assign students to complete the walkthrough in pairs.
2. Use the walkthrough process with a chapter instead of the entire textbook.

BAG OF KNOWLEDGE

ACTIVITY-AT-A-GLANCE

Purpose

Bridge prior knowledge to new information.

When to Use

Use to tie prior knowledge to an upcoming lesson, or use during a lesson to check that students are connecting new information to prior knowledge.

What You'll Need

❑ Paper lunch bags
❑ Index cards

What to Do

1. Give each student a paper lunch bag. List 5 key names, places, events, or concepts from the upcoming lesson.

2. On the outside of the lunch bag, invite students to use words, sketches, or symbols to tell 1 thing they already know about each of the key words or concepts listed. Students may leave a blank if they don't have any ideas for a specific word.

3. After students have answered the questions, arrange them in small groups of 2–4 and have them share what they wrote or drew. As a class, invite students to share what they know about each example.

4. Give each student 5–10 index cards. As the class progresses through the lesson or unit, invite students to write on the cards any new information they learn about the key words or concepts. Students may

IRI/SkyLight Training and Publishing, Inc.

keep the cards inside their lunch bags. At the end of the lesson, have small groups reconvene and invite students to share their bags of new knowledge.

Variations

1. Create an all-class concept map using the key words.
2. Instruct secondary students to create a concept map on their bags.

QUESTION WEB

ACTIVITY-AT-A-GLANCE

Purpose

Clarify key concepts introduced in the first half of a unit.

When to Use

Use in the middle of a lesson or unit to check for student understanding of what they're learning.

What You'll Need

❏ No materials necessary

What to Do

1. Draw a web on the board or overhead and write the unit title in the center.

2. Ask students to review the unit's concepts by volunteering information they have learned. Instruct them to identify parts of the unit for which they need further explanation by constructing questions for any items they do not fully understand.

3. Use a round-robin structure and write each question on the web. After all are posted, work around the web, asking students to suggest answers and recording them next to the corresponding questions. If a student gives a partial answer, ask another volunteer to add to it or to correct it. Answer the questions only when no one else can. Check to make sure everyone understood each answer.

Question Web

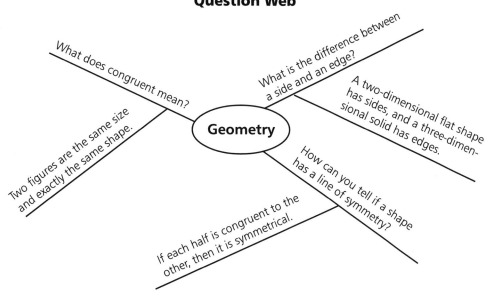

What does congruent mean?

What is the difference between a side and an edge?

Two figures are the same size and exactly the same shape.

Geometry

A two-dimensional flat shape has sides, and a three-dimensional solid has edges.

How can you tell if a shape has a line of symmetry?

If each half is congruent to the other, then it is symmetrical.

Variations

1. Pair students and have them construct a critical question.

2. Identify students who believe they can answer one of the questions. Place each in a separate location in the classroom, and post his or her question. Arrange students in small groups and instruct them to rotate among the student facilitators to discuss each question.

3. List each question on a separate sheet of chart paper and tape sheets around the room. Arrange students in small groups and assign a different group to discuss each question. Have each group decide on an answer and record it under the question. Check for accuracy. Then have the students take a gallery walk, moving from question to question, confirming, expanding on, or correcting answers. Gather as a class to discuss additions and revisions to each answer.

EXPLAIN WHY

Purpose

Extend thinking and expand understanding by elaborating on answers.

When to Use

Use in class discussions in which students tend to give one-word responses.

What You'll Need

❏ No materials necessary

What to Do

1. Arrange students in pairs to complete a task, such as solving a math problem, conducting an experiment, or completing a project. As they work, ask students to record the steps they take.

2. Invite each pair to share its process with the class and explain why each step was necessary. Ask students to tell what steps they would change if they were to attempt the task again and why. Whenever possible, ask for additional explanations.

3. Write a list of "why" questions on the board or overhead. Have pairs answer them and share with the class.

Why Questions

Why are you changing the title of your story?

Why did you decide to work backward to solve that problem?

Why are you rearranging your exercise schedule?

Variations

1. Have a "why" marathon. Join 2 or 3 pairs to see how many "why" questions each group can list about the topic. Then have groups exchange lists and answer as many questions as they can, making sure explanations are thorough.

2. Ask pairs to write out explanations and attach them to their task sheets for grading.

WHAT IT LOOKS LIKE

ACTIVITY-AT-A-GLANCE

Purpose

Develop a process for self-assessment by constructing performance rubrics.

When to Use

Use at the beginning of a task or project to help students develop success criteria for their work. Revisit at the end of the task to help students reflect on and evaluate their work.

What You'll Need

❏ No materials necessary

What to Do

1. On the board or overhead, sketch a T-chart.

2. Select a performance not related to your class, such as taming wild animals or figure skating. Ask the class to brainstorm the actions needed to perform the activity well. Write these criteria, or characteristics of excellence, in the appropriate columns on the T-chart.

3. Have the class vote on the 3 most important criteria for high performance. For example, if a figure skater does a triple axle, what characteristics determine whether he or she has done it well? Height? Revolutions? Balance?

4. Arrange students in 3 groups and assign 1 characteristic to each group. Invite each group to create a rubric for its characteristic that

details 4 levels, or indicators, of success. Have each group explain its rubric to the class.

5. Arrange students in small groups and explain the new task for the lesson at hand. Invite each group to brainstorm 3 criteria for the new task and to create rubrics for each. Review the steps:

   • Identify 3 characteristics of excellence.

   • Find 4 indicators of success for each characteristic.

   • Chart the indicators.

6. After students create rubrics, have them complete the task for the lesson. Invite them to use their rubrics to help them reflect on their work. Discuss how the rubrics helped them complete the task. Discuss how else they might use a rubric to improve their school performance. In future assignments that require students to demonstrate or use knowledge in a performance, include the preparation and use of a rubric.

Sample Rubric for a Research Project			
1 Accuracy of research needs to be increased, and sources need to be cited.	**2** Project shows evidence of some research, but sources need to be cited.	**3** Project shows evidence of accurate research, and adequate sources are cited.	**4** Project shows evidence of detailed, thorough, accurate research, and many sources are cited.

Variations

1. Reduce the number of criteria and indicators required for the rubric. As students increase their proficiency with rubrics, expand the number of criteria and indicators.

2. Provide the rubric for the students.

LEAD-INS

ACTIVITY-AT-A-GLANCE

Purpose

Develop self-assessment techniques by reflecting on learning.

When to Use

Use after a lesson, unit, or project.

What You'll Need

- ❏ Journal
- ❏ Index cards

What to Do

1. Write a lead-in statement on the board or overhead, such as:
   - *Today, I learned . . .*
   - *In this lesson, I discovered . . .*
   - *In this lesson, I was pleased that I . . .*
   - *In this task, I found it easy (difficult) to . . .*
   - *The most important thing I learned in this lesson was . . .*

   Let students know that they will have the chance to use the lead-in as a way of reflecting about how and what they have learned in a lesson or unit.

2. Share an example of a completed reflection. Explain that this is an open-ended reflection without a correct answer. All that is needed is an honest response. Let students know before they begin to write

whether or not the reflections will be collected. As students become more comfortable with the process, they may take more time and may write lengthier reflections.

Variations

1. Change the lead-in to fit a specific situation and to add variety to lessons.

2. Change the medium. The most common medium is a journal. Have students write in it at the end of the day to summarize the key learning experienced, to evaluate their own performance, or to select favorite learning experiences.

3. Have students attach completed reflections to assignments as a way of assessing what they learned or how well they succeeded.

4. Use index cards and collect the completed statements.

5. Instead of written reflections, arrange students in small groups and use lead-in statements as discussion starters.

END QUOTES

ACTIVITY-AT-A-GLANCE

Purpose

Select the most important material or concepts learned in a lesson and construct an evaluative summary.

When to Use

Use at the end of a lesson in order for students to evaluate what they learned and to identify points that may need reinforcing or reviewing.

What You'll Need

- ❏ Chart paper
- ❏ Index cards
- ❏ Journals

What to Do

1. On sheets of chart paper taped to the classroom walls, write the following statements and questions:

   - *What is the most important thing you learned in this lesson?*
   - *What did you like most about this lesson?*
   - *What did you like least about this lesson?*
   - *What did you learn in this lesson that will help you in other classes?*
   - *A contribution I made to the class during this lesson was . . .*
   - *What I learned in this lesson will help me because . . .*

2. Invite each student to choose a statement and move to its location. Students at each location will form a group. Try to get a comparable number of students at each position. Invite each group to think of as many true endings for its statement as possible in 3 minutes. Have a group recorder list all the ideas.

3. After 3 minutes, invite the groups to rotate to the next statement's position and repeat the process. Rotate several times before asking students to return to their seats.

4. Ask each student to write about one of the statements his or her group discussed. Have students put quotation marks around statements to denote that they are direct quotes. Instruct them to edit and sign their cards before turning them in.

Variations

1. Instead of rotating the groups, call for a random remix.

2. Reseat the students in base groups or some other configuration and instruct each group to write the summary together. Collect and read each group's summary.

LETTER TO THE EDITOR

ACTIVITY-AT-A-GLANCE

Purpose

Develop and support a point of view through letter writing.

When to Use

Use in the middle or at the end of a unit to assess what students have learned.

What You'll Need

❏ Examples of letters to a newspaper or magazine editor

What to Do

1. Show students an example of a letter to the editor of a newspaper or magazine that takes a point of view related to the unit's content. For example, if the topic is "pollution in the environment," show a letter taking a point of view about pollution in the local community. If the topic is *To Kill a Mockingbird*, show a letter taking a point of view about treating others with fairness.

2. After showing the letter, discuss how to write a point-of-view letter. Remind students that they need to explain their points of view using facts or research to support their thinking.

3. Brainstorm with students possible issues that relate to the unit, and have each student write a letter expressing his or her opinion about an issue. Use peer editing to review the letters, and then invite students to read their letters aloud.

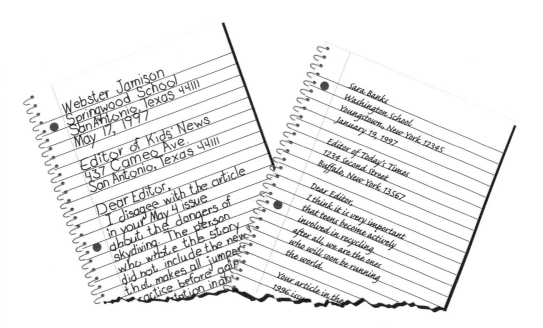

Webster Jamison
Springwood School
San Antonio, Texas 44111
May 17, 1997

Editor of Kids' News
437 Cameo Ave.
San Antonio, Texas 44111

Dear Editor,
I disagree with the article
in your May 4 issue
about the dangers of
skydiving. The person
who wrote the story
did not include the new
that makes all jumpers
ractice before go
lation in an

Sara Banks
Washington School
Youngstown, New York 12345
January 19, 1997

Editor of Today's Times
1234 Second Street
Buffalo, New York 13567

Dear Editor,
I think it is very important
that teens become actively
involved in recycling.
after all, we are the ones
who will soon be running
the world.

Your article in the
1996 issu

Variations

1. Instead of grading the letters, write a brief response to each letter.

2. Pair students with contrasting or different points of view and ask them to write a response to each other's letter.

3. Instead of grading the letters, help students complete a final edit and encourage each student to send his or her letter to the editor of the local newspaper.

4. If used in the middle of a unit, have students predict what the remainder of the unit will cover.

PRACTICAL MATTERS

ACTIVITY-AT-A-GLANCE

Purpose

Synthesize the relevance of a topic in everyday life and apply new information to a real world issue through editorial writing.

When to Use

Use with a topic that has relevance for your students in order to help them process what they have learned.

What You'll Need

❏ Examples of editorials
❏ A rubric or list of criteria for evaluating student-written editorials

What to Do

1. After the class has completed work on a topic, arrange students in small heterogeneous groups. Ask each group to write a paragraph that synthesizes what the students have learned. Review the essays and read aloud 2 or 3 that capture the core ideas of the topic. Encourage each group to rewrite and improve its paragraph.

2. Remix the groups. Ask groups to brainstorm why this topic is important for them to study and list authentic situations in which they might need to apply the new information. Generate a class list from each group's ideas.

3. Show a model editorial. Discuss the format and the elements of a well-written editorial:

Natural Resources

1. If we don't learn to conserve, we won't be able to support life on this planet.
2. We could invent new kinds of fuels that don't pollute.
3. We need to find a way to eliminate garbage and waste.
4. We need to be aware of how much water we are using.

- States the problem or concern.
- States the writer's opinion or point of view.
- Elaborates, providing supporting facts.
- Closes with a concluding statement.

4. Give students a rubric or list of criteria for a successful editorial that you will use to evaluate the completed works. Ask each student to write an editorial on the importance of the topic that the class has been studying, using the list of criteria or the rubric as a guide.

Variations

1. For intermediate or middle school students, assign a 5-paragraph format.
2. Work individually rather than in groups to complete all steps of this process.

DEMOCRATIC DOTS

ACTIVITY-AT-A-GLANCE

Purpose

Use a nonverbal voting system to reach consensus in the assessment of important vocabulary in a lesson or unit.

When to Use

Use to determine the most important vocabulary words for a lesson or unit and to emphasize connections between the vocabulary and the lesson's goals.

What You'll Need

❑ Dot stickers
❑ Chart paper

What to Do

1. Arrange students into heterogeneous groups of 5 and provide students with chart paper. Explain that each group should make a list of the 10 most important vocabulary words studied and their definitions and review the meanings of the selected words.

2. Give each student 3 dot stickers. Ask students to vote for the 3 most important words on their group's list by placing the dots next to their choices. Before voting, group members may debate for 5 minutes. After all have placed their dots, have groups total the results.

3. Make an all-class list of the winning words from each small group. Repeat the dot process until a top 10 list for the class is created.

Important Vocabulary

- •• prejudice — prejudging
- ••• The <u>North Star</u> — newspaper begun by Frederick Douglass
- • orator — public speaker
- • amendment — addition to the Constitution
- •••• abolition — eliminate slavery
- ••• underground railroad — a movement that helped slaves escape
- • liberate — to free

Variations

1. For primary students, use a smaller-sized group and a shorter list of words.

2. Conclude the top 10 list by requiring all students to recall the correct spelling, the meaning in context, and a reason why the selected words are the most important to the lesson or unit.

3. Have students use a different medium (e.g., collage, pantomime, mobile) to communicate the relation of the top 10 words to the lesson or unit goals.

GOLDFISH BOWL

ACTIVITY-AT-A-GLANCE

Purpose

Read for the understanding of key concepts and learn from listening.

When to Use

Use when teaching concepts from textbooks or other written sources.

What You'll Need

- ❏ Cardboard fish figures
- ❏ Bowl
- ❏ Checklist of presentation requirements

What to Do

1. Cut out several small cardboard fish figures and write a subheading from the textbook chapter on each. Put all fish in a bowl.

2. After students have read the chapter, arrange them in small groups (or pairs). Allow each group to choose a fish from the bowl, which indicates the section of the chapter for which the group is responsible. Each group is to:

   - Summarize the key idea of its section.
   - Explain the meaning of new vocabulary or important facts.
   - Explain how its section fits into the main idea of the chapter.

3. Invite each group to present its section to the class. Ask listeners to use a checklist to assess how well the presentations cover the material according to the 3 requirements. In addition, the audience should take notes during each presentation in preparation for a class discussion and review of the chapter.

4. Close by asking students how the presentations helped them identify the key components to study in the chapter.

Variations

1. Make and label a fish for each student in the class and then have students who chose similar sections form into groups.

2. Have each student work independently to write a summary for his or her section.

3. After a demonstration chapter is completed, assign students to cover an entire chapter.

RANK ORDERING

ACTIVITY-AT-A-GLANCE

Purpose

Identify the relative importance of one item to another.

When to Use

Use in the middle or at the end of a lesson or unit when helping students distinguish and prioritize the importance or value of information and concepts learned.

What You'll Need

❏ No materials necessary

What to Do

1. Brainstorm with the class a list of concepts or items that students are to assess, such as the characters in a novel, problem-solving methods, or causes leading to a historic event.

2. Have students vote to determine the 3 most important items on the list in relation to the main idea of the lesson or unit. Explain that each student should vote a total of 3 times. They begin with closed fists, but as the list of items is read aloud, they hold up 1 finger to indicate a first-place vote, 2 fingers to indicate a second-place vote, and 3 fingers to indicate a third-place vote.

3. A class recorder tallies the votes and writes the score beside each item. A final count will give the rank order. Conclude with a class discussion of the top 3 choices, eliciting from students their reasons for choosing them.

IRI/SkyLight Training and Publishing, Inc.

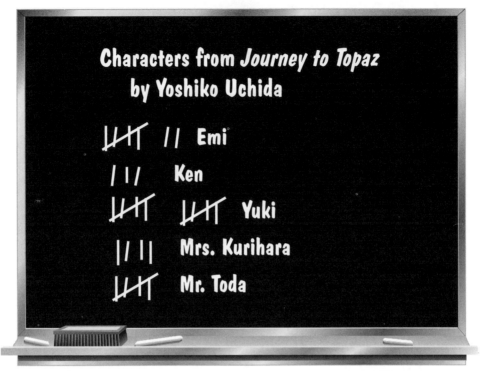

Characters from *Journey to Topaz*
by Yoshiko Uchida

||||| || Emi

/ | / Ken

||||| ||||| Yuki

|/ || Mrs. Kurihara

||||| Mr. Toda

Variations

1. Use straight voting of 1 vote per person. The final rank depends on which items have the most votes.

2. Before voting, have students debate the issues, explaining the reasoning behind each of their first choices.

EXEMPLARY EXAMPLES

ACTIVITY-AT-A-GLANCE

Purpose

Use narrative examples to illustrate concepts.

When to Use

Use when developing expository or narrative writing and when introducing public speaking.

What You'll Need

❏ No materials necessary

What to Do

1. Brainstorm with students a list of characters from a novel or famous persons studied in previous units. For each, highlight his or her key character attributes, such as honesty and hard working or sneaky and deceitful.

2. Tell a sample personal story to illustrate one of the attributes. Discuss the advantages of using a narrative example.

3. Invite 1 or 2 volunteers to tell similar stories to the class. Identify the strengths of each student's example.

4. Ask each student to select 1 attribute from the list and write a personal story or paragraph to illustrate that attribute. Discuss the criteria for the stories in advance or provide students with a rubric.

5. Collect and provide feedback for each story.

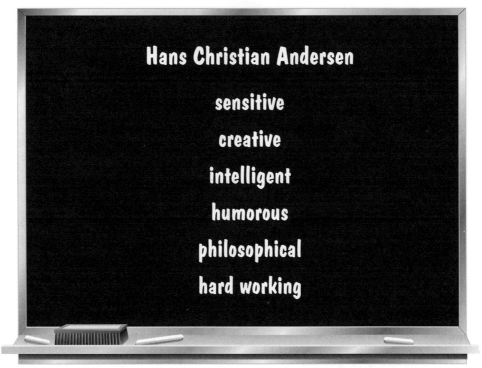

Hans Christian Andersen

sensitive

creative

intelligent

humorous

philosophical

hard working

Variations

1. Use a web or matrix for detailing character attributes.

2. Have students illustrate unit concepts by telling personal or narrative stories.

3. Instead of providing students with the criteria for a quality story or paragraph, have students brainstorm standards for success.

4. Use a peer-editing system for revising paragraphs.

5. Invite students to share their stories in small groups or by reading aloud to the class.

FIVE PARAGRAPHS PLUS

ACTIVITY-AT-A-GLANCE

Purpose

Understand the basic design of a 5-paragraph expository essay.

When to Use

Use when introducing the structure of an expository essay or when emphasizing the importance of providing supporting facts for ideas in an essay.

What You'll Need

❑ Picture of 3-legged stool

What to Do

1. Show students a picture of a 3-legged stool. Explain the metaphor of the stool in relation to a well-organized essay with a central or main idea (the seat), supporting examples (the legs), and conclusion (surface stool sits on).

2. Draw the 3-legged stool on the board or overhead and write an example of a main idea, its 3 supporting ideas, and a conclusion in the appropriate parts. Use the example to model how to write a 5-paragraph essay that includes an introductory paragraph, 3 supporting paragraphs, and a concluding paragraph.

3. Discuss the criteria for the essays in advance or provide students with a rubric. You may want to include grammar, punctuation,

The United States Government
(Main Idea)

Executive Branch
(Supporting Idea)

Legislative Branch
(Supporting Idea)

Judicial Branch
(Supporting Idea)

Balance in Democratic Government
(Concluding Paragraph)

sentence structure, and spelling criteria as well as the number of detail sentences per paragraph, interest, and accuracy of information.

4. Provide feedback based on established criteria. Discuss the best essays with the class.

Variations

1. Use peer-review teams comprised of students who are familiar with the basic 5-paragraph structure to critique outlines and drafts.

2. Emphasize the steps in the writing process by providing due dates for each stage (outline or prewriting, first draft, revision, and final edit).

CONCEPT CONNECTIONS

ACTIVITY-AT-A-GLANCE

Purpose

Develop words and phrases that bridge ideas in writing.

When to Use

Use when guiding students to improve expository, persuasive, or narrative writing.

What You'll Need

❑ Copies of Bridging Ideas
❑ Sample essay that uses bridging words
❑ Books and magazines
❑ Picture of a bridge (optional)

What to Do

1. Show students a picture of a bridge (or draw one on the board) and ask them to explain its purpose. Use the bridge as a metaphor for words or phrases that connect ideas in writing.

2. Show a 3-paragraph essay that uses bridging words. Discuss how the author used language to connect ideas. Explain to students that they will be looking in books and magazines to find examples of bridging words.

Bridging Ideas

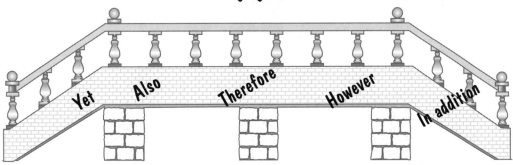

3. Provide each student with a copy of Bridging Ideas. Invite students to choose a book or magazine and to look for the words that the author used to bridge, or connect, ideas. Ask students to write the words and phrases they find on their copies of Bridging Ideas. Invite volunteers to share their words and read the passages in which they found them.

4. Assign a 3–5 paragraph essay. Establish a criterion that calls for appropriate use of bridging words.

5. Use a peer-editing system for reviewing the words used and revising paragraphs.

Variations

1. Create an all-class list of bridging words and post for reference throughout the year.

2. Find examples of bridging words in class textbooks.

3. Use after students have written an essay. Ask students to review their essays and find any bridging words they used. Have students identify 1–3 examples where they could use bridging words and rewrite those sentences using bridging words.

NEWSPAPER GRAPHIC

ACTIVITY-AT-A-GLANCE

Purpose

Use a visual format for compiling information and organizing an expository essay or narrative.

When to Use

Use when introducing expository essays or the key components of a news story.

What You'll Need

- ❏ One newspaper article per group
- ❏ Chart paper
- ❏ Copies of The Newspaper Model

What to Do

1. Arrange students into groups of 3. Assign cooperative group roles: 1 student is the reader, 1 is the recorder, and 1 is the encourager (who makes sure each student has an opportunity to speak).

2. Provide each group with a newspaper article and a large sheet of chart paper labeled with the following headings: who, what, when, where, why, and how. Instruct students to read the articles and list the facts that they find under the appropriate headings.

3. Post the completed lists with their corresponding articles at different locations around the room. Rotate groups from station to station so that students can discuss several of the articles and lists of facts. Review 2–3 examples with the class. Ask volunteers to explain why the 6 questions are important.

                                    IRI/SkyLight Training and Publishing, Inc.

The Newspaper Model

Topic: The Boston Tea Party

Who	What	When	Where	Why	How
Patriots	American Revolution	1776	Boston, MA	Rebel against "taxation without representation"	Disposed of tea in harbor

Write a paragraph using the information from this inverted pyramid form.

In Boston, in the late 1700s, the Patriots, who were colonists opposing the British government, protested the issue of "taxation without representation." They disposed of a shipment of tea by dumping it overboard into the harbor. This event, among others, led to the American Revolutionary War, in which we gained our independence as a nation.

4. Explain to students that they will be writing their own newspaper articles. Brainstorm a list of current school and community events that could be used as topics. Select 1 topic to use as an example. Model listing facts for each of the 6 headings on The Newspaper Model and writing a paragraph using those facts.

5. Invite each student to choose a topic, complete a copy of The Newspaper Model, and write his or her own article. Provide corrective feedback on the completed articles and review 2–3 samples with the class, pointing out the strengths of each.

6. Invite students to reflect on their experience using The Newspaper Model by listing the pluses, minuses, and intriguing aspects (PMI) of using this graphic organizer.

Variations

1. Students can remain in their original groups for steps 4–6.

2. Use peer-editing pairs for the revising and editing stages of the writing process.

3. Ask students to think of other classes or subjects for which this graphic organizer could be helpful.

STORY TREE

ACTIVITY-AT-A-GLANCE

Purpose

Use a graphic organizer to identify and list the major elements of a story.

When to Use

Use when introducing or expanding students' abilities to analyze fiction according to the elements of a story.

What You'll Need

❑ Copies of Story Tree

What to Do

1. Invite volunteers to identify the elements of a story (characters, setting, theme, events, conflicts). Work together to clarify the terms.

2. Give students copies of Story Tree. Invite them to use the graphic organizer as they read a short story or part of a novel. Have students record examples on the tree as they identify specific elements.

3. After all students have read the selection, project a blank copy of Story Tree on the overhead or draw it on the board. Invite students to volunteer examples of each element and complete the story tree as a class. Make sure the class agrees with the placement of the ideas. If there is a disagreement, encourage discussion.

4. Ask each student to write a summary paragraph about one of the story's elements, such as its characters. Before students begin to write, review the criteria for a good summation.

IRI/SkyLight Training and Publishing, Inc.

20

Story Tree

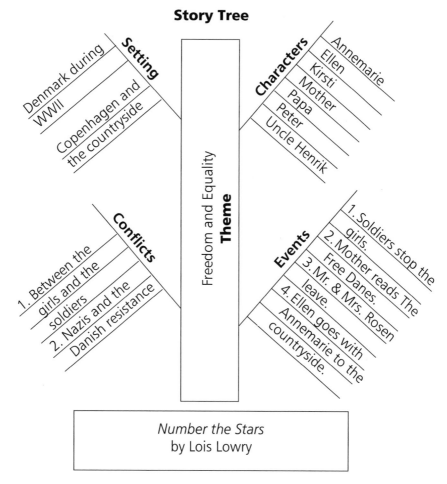

Setting
- Denmark during WWII
- Copenhagen and the countryside

Characters
- Annemarie
- Ellen
- Kirsti
- Mother
- Papa
- Peter
- Uncle Henrik

Theme
Freedom and Equality

Conflicts
1. Between the girls and the soldiers
2. Nazis and the Danish resistance

Events
1. Soldiers stop the girls.
2. Mother reads The Free Danes.
3. Mr. & Mrs. Rosen leave.
4. Ellen goes with Annemarie to the countryside.

Number the Stars
by Lois Lowry

5. Invite students to tell what they have learned about the elements of a story.

Variations

1. Delay recording on the story trees until the entire story is read.
2. For primary and intermediate students, substitute problem and solution for the conflict element.

CLASS MAGAZINE

ACTIVITY-AT-A-GLANCE

Purpose

Gain experience in creating stories, articles, and ads while writing for an authentic reason.

When to Use

Use to motivate student writing at any time during the year.

What You'll Need

❑ Age-appropriate magazines
❑ Duplicating equipment and materials

What to Do

1. Give pairs of students age-appropriate magazines. (Different editions are fine.) Ask pairs to formulate a list of the magazine's components, such as the cover, table of contents, stories, articles, interviews, features, and ads. Discuss whether each component is found in every magazine or if it is found only in some.

2. Explain class assignment: to create a class magazine. Appoint or elect students to the following jobs: editor-in-chief, associate editors, story writers, feature writers, graphic artists, ad writers, photographers (need cameras), and proofreaders.

3. Assign tasks and deadlines for each component. Hold a meeting to determine the class magazine's focus, theme, title, and each person's responsibilities.

   IRI/SkyLight Training and Publishing, Inc.

21

4. As each student revises his or her work, conference with individuals to ensure quality. Help the students assemble all the parts and, if possible, duplicate copies of the completed magazine for every student.

5. Close with a discussion of problems that students may have encountered and the solutions they invented while working on the tasks.

Variations

1. Arrange students in teams of 5–7, and have each team create its own magazine. Identify the similarities and differences among the groups' different products.

2. Provide or develop a list of criteria for a good magazine, for well-written articles, and for ads. Use the criteria to assess individual work and the completed magazine.

INTERVIEWING

ACTIVITY-AT-A-GLANCE

Purpose

Develop questioning skills while gaining insight into the difference between closed and open-ended questions.

When to Use

Use when introducing a unit involving famous persons, when studying biographies, or when investigating characters in literature.

What You'll Need

❑ Copies of Three-Story Intellect Verbs

What to Do

1. Discuss the difference between a closed question that elicits factual, right or wrong answers and an open-ended question that elicits a variety of different responses.

2. Show the class the Three-Story Intellect Verbs diagram. Using the metaphor of a house, explain that the first story on the diagram shows verbs for factual, or closed, questions. The second story shows verbs for open-ended questions that elicit answers involving comparing, reasoning, and generalizing, in addition to knowing the facts. The third story lists verbs for open-ended questions that invite imagining, predicting, and idealizing. Each level of question builds on the level before it. Explain that students will be developing interviews using these 3 types of questions and may use the listed verbs or any others that they choose.

Three-Story Intellect Verbs

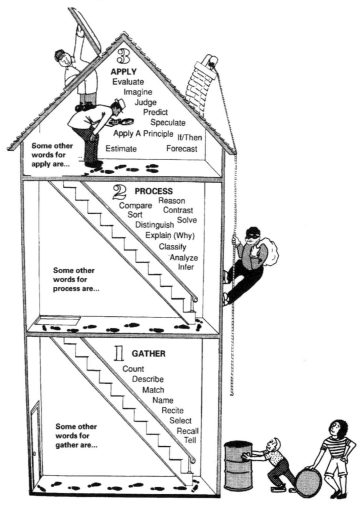

③ APPLY
Evaluate
Imagine
Judge
Predict
Speculate
Apply A Principle   If/Then
Estimate   Forecast

Some other words for apply are...

② PROCESS
Reason
Compare   Contrast
Sort   Solve
Distinguish
Explain (Why)
Classify
Analyze
Infer

Some other words for process are...

① GATHER
Count
Describe
Match
Name
Recite
Select
Recall
Tell

Some other words for gather are...

3. Create a list of famous people (or characters) related to the unit's topic or whom the students would like to investigate. Choose one to use as a sample for modeling questioning strategies. Invite volunteers to pretend they are interviewing the person and to ask sample questions. Have each student explain the level (according to the diagram) at which his or her question would be categorized.

Questions for Helen Keller

1. How old were you when you learned to sign? (level 1)

2. If you could live your life over, what would you change? (level 3)

4. Arrange students in pairs. Invite each pair to select 1 name from the class list and to prepare 2 closed and 4 open-ended questions about that person.

5. Join pairs into groups of 4 students each. Have students share their interview questions and jointly decide the level of each question.

6. Have volunteers share their questions and explanations with the class. Invite students to tell what they learned about asking questions.

Variations

1. Have students discuss authentic situations or class activities in which the different levels of questions would be most useful.

2. Use the diagram for a homework assignment. Instruct students to observe the kinds of questions their reports or essays answer.

3. Have younger students work with only 2 levels of questions: factual and those that involve comparing, reasoning, and generalizing.

Ideas

TV NEWS FLASH

ACTIVITY-AT-A-GLANCE

Purpose

Develop narrative, persuasive, and presentation skills while demonstrating knowledge on a topic.

When to Use

Use in the middle or at the end of a unit.

What You'll Need

❏ Videotapes of news shows, VCR
❏ Copies of The Newspaper Model

What to Do

1. Play videotaped segments of TV news shows from different channels. Ask students to rate each segment on a 1–5 scale and to explain their reasoning. From their explanations, extract 3–5 criteria for judging the quality of content and presentation.

2. Provide students with copies of The Newspaper Model and invite each to write a school-based news story. Explain that students will be creating their own news broadcasts. Review the students' drafts before they present and encourage appropriate changes.

3. Create a set for the class news station. Schedule presentations on successive days and assess each using class-developed criteria.

4. After the last presentation, discuss the overall pluses and minuses of the performances.

IRI/SkyLight Training and Publishing, Inc.

Variations

1. Use teams of 5 to copy the style of a specific station's news show.
2. Invite a news anchor or TV reporter from a local channel to speak to the class about his or her job.
3. Write letters to news anchors or TV reporters asking questions about their jobs. Invite them to respond to students' letters by enclosing a self-addressed, stamped envelope.
4. Videotape student presentations and play them for parents during open house.

RESPONSE IN TURN

ACTIVITY-AT-A-GLANCE

Purpose

Contribute while working in large and small groups.

When to Use

Use after completing a task, lesson, or unit.

What You'll Need

❏ No materials necessary

What to Do

1. Invite students to summarize key points in a lesson or unit by:

   • Completing a lead-in statement, such as *In this lesson, I was pleased that . . .*

   • Answering an open-ended question, such as *If you were to imagine a different outcome, what would it be?*

   • Listing the pluses, minuses, and intriguing aspects (PMI) of the lesson.

2. Allow students time to think before inviting volunteers to share their responses. Encourage different answers and active listening. If appropriate, ask clarifying questions.

3. In a large class, vary the statement or question after every 7–8 students.

4. Ask a volunteer to summarize the responses.

Variations

1. Use the technique in small groups and have 1 student from each group summarize or highlight the group's responses for the class. After all groups have responded, conclude with a final summary.
2. Allow each student to write a response on a card and read it in turn.

SOLVE A STORY

ACTIVITY-AT-A-GLANCE

Purpose

Identify problems in a story or authentic situation and determine best solutions.

When to Use

Use during or at the end of a lesson or unit.

What You'll Need

❑ Index cards for note taking
❑ Copies of scenarios (sample scenarios listed in "Blacklines" section)
❑ Copies of Problem-Solving Chart

What to Do

1. As a class, brainstorm a list of favorite television shows and invite students to share why they chose them.

2. On the overhead or board, draw a two-column T-chart with the headings "Problem" and "Strategies to Use." Choose 1 show from the list and invite a volunteer to discuss a problem situation that occurs in the show. Brainstorm possible solutions to the problem and complete the chart.

3. Explain that students will be acting out a problem situation and deciding on a solution to the problem. Arrange students in groups of 3 and assign the following cooperative group roles: reader, recorder, and encourager. The reader will read a scenario aloud. The recorder

Problem	Strategies to Use
Lily needs money to buy her mother a present.	Lily could • Babysit • Work for her grandfather • Ask her uncle for a loan

will take notes on the group's discussion. The encourager will make sure each student has an opportunity to speak.

4. Provide each group with a scenario to dramatize. Have students discuss the situation, identify the problem, and agree upon how they will solve it. Group members should decide who will play each character and then practice the skit. Allow students to use props.

5. Invite groups to present their skits and explain the rationale behind the solutions.

6. Give each group a copy of the Problem-Solving Chart and ask students to work together to complete it.

Variations

1. Select a short story for each group to dramatize.

2. Have 1 member other than the reader summarize the story for the class and a different member explain how the group used problem solving in the task.

Problem-Solving Chart

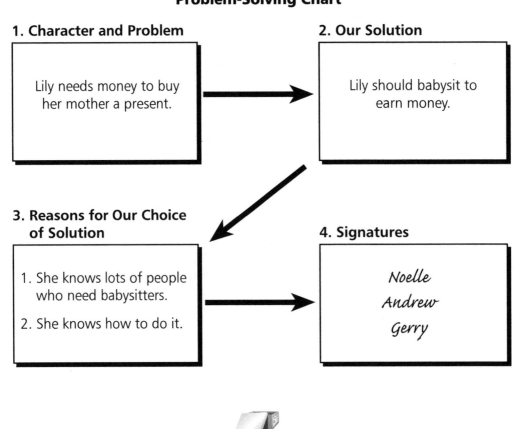

1. Character and Problem

Lily needs money to buy her mother a present.

2. Our Solution

Lily should babysit to earn money.

3. Reasons for Our Choice of Solution

1. She knows lots of people who need babysitters.
2. She knows how to do it.

4. Signatures

Noelle

Andrew

Gerry

IRI/SkyLight Training and Publishing, Inc.

LOGICAL/ MATHEMATICAL

IMPROVEMENT RUBRIC

ACTIVITY-AT-A-GLANCE

Purpose

Learn specific criteria for improving mathematical skills as identified in a guide or rubric of criteria and indicators.

When to Use

Use before, during, and following a lesson.

What You'll Need

❑ Model rubric

What to Do

1. Provide a model rubric for all to see. Be sure that the model details the key skills students will develop in the lesson or unit.
2. Walk students through the model rubric. Check for understanding.
3. Keep the model rubric posted during the unit.
4. Use the model rubric during the unit to conference with students and mark progress.
5. Provide a completed rubric for each student to be used at parent conferences.

Math Skills: Long Division

Criteria	1	2	3	4
Accurate	Few Correct	Some Correct	Most Correct	All Correct
Process Steps Clearly Used	Doesn't Know Steps	Skips Steps	Most Correct	All Correct
Work Is Checked	Never	Seldom	Often	Always

Variations

1. Ask students to identify criteria to be used in the rubric.
2. Have students create individual rubrics for specific tasks and use them as self-assessment tools upon completion of the task(s).

PEOPLE SEARCH

ACTIVITY-AT-A-GLANCE

Purpose

Access prior knowledge when being introduced to a new topic in mathematics.

When to Use

Use when introducing students to a math topic or a unit in another subject area, or as an icebreaker with a new class.

What You'll Need

❑ Copies of People Search

What to Do

1. Use the blank People Search to create a scavenger-hunt activity that relates to your topic or unit. Complete the statements in each square to provide clues as shown in the sample on the next page.

2. Distribute a copy of your newly created People Search to each student and explain the rules:

   • In 10 minutes, students must obtain a signature for as many of the squares as possible.

   • Students must first introduce themselves before asking for correct answers.

   • Students may use the signature of each student only once.

   • When students have obtained a signature for every square, they should return to their seats.

People Search

Find a Person Who . . .

1. has cut a pie into equal-sized pieces. _____	2. has broken a limb. _____	3. can find the sum of $\frac{1}{4} + \frac{1}{2}$. _____
4. knows how many nickels are in one dollar. _____	5. has used a recipe with fractions. _____	6. knows who said, "A job half done is well begun." _____
7. can tell how many students are in one fifth of this class. _____	8. can multiply $\frac{5}{2} \times \frac{2}{5}$ correctly. _____	9. who knows which is larger, $\frac{8}{32}$ or $\frac{5}{16}$. _____

3. At the end of 10 minutes, ask for volunteers to share some of the responses they recorded.

4. Introduce the new unit's topic and bridge from what students already know to what they will be studying.

Variations

1. Use the search at the end of a lesson to tie knowledge together.

2. When students have completed their searches, invite them to make up new questions for their own People Search.

MATH JIGSAW

ACTIVITY-AT-A-GLANCE

Purpose

Complete a variety of practice problems presented in a lesson.

When to Use

Use during guided practice and with a range of problems before independent practice. Use with students who benefit from sequential, step-by-step instruction or from working in a mixed-ability group.

What You'll Need

❏ No materials necessary

What to Do

1. After providing direct instruction on a math topic, divide the class into pairs or trios.

2. Divide the number of practice problems for the assignment by the number of pairs or trios. Assign problems to each group.

3. Guide the practice with coaching appropriate to each group. Insist that all group members know how to explain their problem-solving methods, step by step.

4. Identify and reteach concepts needing clarification. Highlight correct procedures.

Variations

1. With same-ability groups, assign practice problems that are the appropriate level of difficulty.
2. Assign 2 pairs of students the same set of practice problems. After each pair completes its work, invite pairs to check each other's work.

SEQUENCE CHART

ACTIVITY-AT-A-GLANCE

Purpose

Organize the steps for solving a problem and build analytical thinking skills through the use of the problem-solving process.

When to Use

Use at the beginning of a lesson or unit involving problem solving.

What You'll Need

❑ Index cards
❑ Sequence chart of the problem-solving process

What to Do

1. Review the steps for solving a math problem using the problem-solving process and post the steps in a sequence chart. Write key words or phrases for each step on 5 x 8 index cards.

2. Check for understanding by removing different cards and asking students to tell what steps are missing.

3. Arrange students in pairs or small groups. Give each group a word problem to solve and a set of 5 index cards. As they complete each step, have students label the front of an index card with the step completed and on the back of the card explain the math step for their specific problem.

4. Select a group of students to model how they solved their problem. Instruct them to tape their work to the displayed sequence chart and explain why they chose to complete each step the way they did.

The Problem-Solving Process

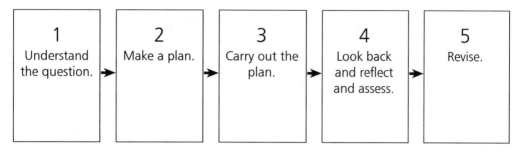

| 1 Understand the question. | 2 Make a plan. | 3 Carry out the plan. | 4 Look back and reflect and assess. | 5 Revise. |

5. Assign additional problems to be solved using the sequence chart.

Variations

1. Instead of having students label the problem-solving steps on their index cards, have them write only the explanation for each step. Then ask each group to mix up its set of completed cards and exchange it with another group's set. Ask students to then put their new set of cards in the correct sequential order and to name each problem-solving step.

2. Test for individual knowledge of the process sequence by mixing up the steps and inviting students to rearrange them to show the proper order.

3. Shorten or lengthen the number of steps based on the readiness of the students.

PAIRED-PARTNER PROBLEM SOLVING

ACTIVITY-AT-A-GLANCE

Purpose

Apply the mathematical problem-solving process.

When to Use

Use throughout a unit or lesson to help students review the explicit steps necessary for problem solving.

What You'll Need

❏ No materials necessary

What to Do

1. Review the problem-solving process and check for student ability to follow the steps.

2. Arrange students in pairs and assign 2 problems to each pair. Explain that one student is to solve problem 1, identifying the problem-solving steps as he or she completes them. The other student is to record the first student's thinking.

3. Monitor student work and coach as needed.

4. Instruct students to repeat the process for the second problem but to reverse their roles.

5. Invite 2–3 pairs to demonstrate their problem-solving steps for the class. Ask questions to mediate accuracy and complete use of the process.

Step 1
What is the problem asking me to find out?

How many miles per gallon the car uses

Step 2
My plan

Take the total number of miles the car traveled and divide it by the number of gallons it used

6. Reteach any steps with which students have difficulty. Remix partners, assign 2 new problems to each pair, and repeat the problem-solving sequence.

Variations

1. Use the problem-solving process after the students finish a problem to assess their thinking.

2. Invite pairs of students to create a math puzzle by writing the steps to solve a problem and leaving out some steps. Have different pairs try to determine the missing steps.

PIZZA PIZZA

ACTIVITY-AT-A-GLANCE

Purpose

Apply basic computational skills to practical situations.

When to Use

Use throughout a unit to practice using the problem-solving process in a variety of authentic situations.

What You'll Need

❑ Chart paper

What to Do

1. On the overhead or board, draw a pizza. Invite the class to brainstorm possible math problems (e.g., cost for one pizza multiplied by the number of pizzas for a class; whole cost vs. piece cost; cost of ingredients plus labor vs. profit margin; gross margin vs. net after taxes).

2. Create groups of 2–3 students and provide each group with a sheet of chart paper. Demonstrate how to write one- and two-step word problems. Check for understanding and invite each group to create its own word problem and write it on the chart paper.

3. Ask each group to exchange its problem with another group for solving.

4. Invite students to share their methods for solving the problems, and have the original groups check computation. Discuss what students learned from creating the word problems.

Variations

1. Have students think of other practical situations that involve steps, such as making a pair of jeans, baking a cake, or building a model airplane.

2. Have students set up problems involving money. Have students use play dollars and coins to solve them, recording the steps they take.

GRAPH IT

ACTIVITY-AT-A-GLANCE

Purpose

Practice making graphs.

When to Use

Use throughout a lesson or unit to practice graph making, enrich presentations, or calculate choices and preferences in a number survey.

What You'll Need

❏ Graph paper

What to Do

1. Select the type of graph for this assignment.
2. Use a survey or other collected results from the classroom (e.g., wall length, number of desks, etc.).
3. On the board or overhead, show a sample graph for all to see. Note its parameters.
4. Check for understanding and ask each student to develop a similar graph of his or her choice.

Favorite Subjects

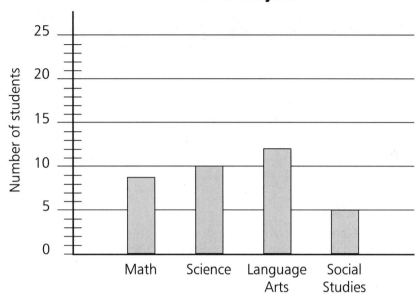

Variations

1. Change the type of graph (e.g., bar, line, pie).
2. Change the number content.
3. Incorporate graphs into a written report or verbal presentation.

NUMBER SURVEY

ACTIVITY-AT-A-GLANCE

Purpose

Use surveys of familiar items as a basis for calculation.

When to Use

Use at the beginning of a lesson or unit to prepare students for gathering data or to introduce statistics as a tool.

What You'll Need

❏ Calculators

What to Do

1. On the board or overhead, show samples of number-based survey questions (e.g., How many students are in the class? How tall is a favorite tree?).

2. Ask the class to brainstorm some number-based questions they might ask their family members. List these.

3. Select 6 questions for each student to ask his or her family.

4. Construct a tally sheet for each question. Divide the class into 6 groups. Assign each group to tally 1 set of responses.

5. Show students how to calculate. Use:
   - Range: difference between highest and lowest number.
   - Mode: number recurring most often.
   - Median: middle number of a set in numerical order.
   - Mean or average: the sum of all numbers divided by the number of units.
6. Invite students to calculate and make verbal conclusions based on the results.

Variations

1. Make the number surveys more or less complex based on student ability.
2. Combine with a science or social studies issue to gather statistical data for a hypothesis.

SCALE IT

ACTIVITY-AT-A-GLANCE

Purpose

Scale objects.

When to Use

Use at the beginning of a lesson or unit to introduce proportion and scale or use throughout a unit to provide the foundation for more complex problems of scale.

What You'll Need

❑ Grids
❑ Rulers

What to Do

1. Ask students what they know about the word "scale" (e.g., fish scales, weight scales, to measure proportion).
2. Identify the scale they will work with.
3. Investigate the word "proportion." What does it mean when it is associated with scale?
4. Present a grid in a scale of 10' x 20' with each square 1" x 1". Indicate the size of each square and ask students to determine the grid size.
5. Tell students that the grid represents a classroom. Provide each student with a ruler to measure the size of his or her desk and place it on the grid in proportion.

IRI/SkyLight Training and Publishing, Inc.

6. Ask students to calculate how many desks can fit in a 10' x 20' classroom with at least 30 percent of the space not used for student desks. Have students discuss how they solved the problem.

7. Discuss the meaning and value of proportion.

Variations

1. Do the measurement tasks in pairs.

2. Provide scaled cutouts for arrangement on the grid.

3. Invite cooperative teams to measure furniture in the classroom or at home and to scale these on a grid.

PIE CHART

ACTIVITY-AT-A-GLANCE

Purpose

Use the pie chart as a tool for calculating percentages.

When to Use

Use prior to conducting a survey or when beginning a research project.

What You'll Need

❏ No materials necessary

What to Do

1. Show a pie chart on the board or overhead. Invite 3 students to agree on how much "pie" each can eat. Mark the answers.

2. Do a second pie chart. Invite 4 students to "eat some pie" and mark their answers.

3. Explain the pie chart. Show students how they can use it to illustrate statistical results.

4. Assign a statistical task in another content area such as social studies. Require the use of a pie chart to display results.

How much homework should 7th graders have every night?

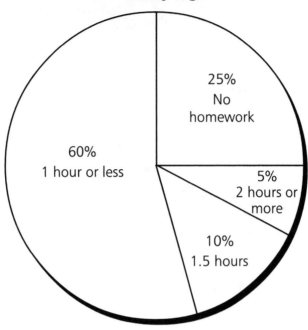

25%
No
homework

60%
1 hour or less

5%
2 hours or
more

10%
1.5 hours

Variations

1. Increase the number of samples included in the pie chart for variety.
2. Have students work in pairs or trios to create pie charts related to events, opinions, or objects in the classroom.

RECIPE

ACTIVITY-AT-A-GLANCE

Purpose

Use metric and customary English (traditional U.S.) measures of capacity.

When to Use

Use throughout a unit or lesson to practice calculations or to reinforce knowledge of a measurement system.

What You'll Need

- ❏ Recipe and ingredients
- ❏ Cooking utensils
- ❏ Kitchen facilities

What to Do

1. Select a recipe appropriate for students by age and mathematical readiness (e.g., cookies for primary students, soups for middle school students).

2. After teaching the measurement table, provide pairs with copies of the recipe, the ingredients, and the necessary cooking utensils.

3. Demonstrate how to use the recipe. Discuss proper measurements and check for understanding. Combine ingredients and cook. Take time for counting games (e.g., 50 cookies at 1 oz. per cookie equals __) using the prepared items.

4. Eat the snack while discussing what the students learned.

IRI/SkyLight Training and Publishing, Inc.

36

Variations

1. Select increasingly difficult recipes.

2. Work with calculators to change the recipe size.

3. Give different recipes to each group.

4. Ask students to rewrite the recipe by converting customary English measures to metric units or vice versa.

COLLECT, COUNT, AND CLASSIFY

ACTIVITY-AT-A-GLANCE

Purpose

Apply the mathematical skills of counting, attributing, classifying, comparing, and contrasting.

When to Use

Use throughout a unit or lesson to practice counting with real objects, to integrate mathematics with science study, and to practice analytical thinking.

What You'll Need

❏ Several items to classify
❏ Containers, cardboard sheets, pins, glue

What to Do

1. Select an item to classify (e.g., stones, seeds, insects, bark, leaves, feathers). Pick one that is easy for students to scavenge.

2. Provide each student with a small container, a sheet of cardboard, straight pins, and glue.

3. Go on a scavenger hunt to collect the targeted object. After all students have a set number, return to the classroom.

4. Identify attributes of the object that allow classification. Set a minimum number per "class." Arrange the objects by class on the cardboard. Label the classes.

IRI/SkyLight Training and Publishing, Inc.

37

5. Use the classification board for counting tasks (e.g., add class a and class b; divide class c into the total).

6. Discuss the attributes used for forming each class. Note similarities and differences.

Variations

1. Use pairs and trios during the scavenger hunt.

2. Use teams to gather different, specific items.

3. Combine individual collections for "super" calculations.

4. Provide students several related items (e.g., books, buttons). Ask students to sort items into groups based on shared characteristics and to brainstorm as many ways to group items as possible (e.g., books with indexes, hardcover books, books with pictures, books with blue covers).

PATTERNS

ACTIVITY-AT-A-GLANCE

Purpose

Understand the concept of patterns.

When to Use

Use with primary students prior to introducing or reviewing number patterns.

What You'll Need

❑ Legos or building blocks (variety of colors)

What to Do

1. Provide each student with a set of Legos or colored blocks. Each set will need at least 2 colors.

2. Demonstrate how students can make a sequenced pattern using 2 different colors of blocks. Explain the principle of patterns so they don't just copy the example.

3. Ask students to create patterns using the Legos or colored blocks.

4. Invite students to share their constructions with the class and explain the patterns they created.

5. Locate patterns in buildings and other places. Discuss with students.

6. Bridge to number patterns.

Variations

1. Use pairs to make the patterns.

2. Use 3 or 4 different colors to create more complex patterns.

3. Ask students to identify 1–3 examples of patterns in objects found outside the classroom and to either sketch the patterns or write a paragraph describing each pattern.

STOCK EXCHANGE

ACTIVITY-AT-A-GLANCE

Purpose

Think in numerical terms.

When to Use

Use with middle school and secondary students during lessons or units to practice calculations in a real world context.

What You'll Need

❑ Play money
❑ Newspapers, brochures, or magazines containing information on stocks

What to Do

1. Explain to students how the stock market works.

2. Provide each student with $1,000 of artificial cash.

3. Provide students with materials to research stocks such as newspapers, brochures, or financial magazines.

4. Have students "purchase" and record their stock selections.

5. One day a week, have students trade, purchase, or sell stocks and calculate their gains and losses.

6. End the unit after 9 weeks with a discussion about what they learned using mathematics for buying and selling stocks.

IRI/SkyLight Training and Publishing, Inc.

Variations

1. Use teams of 3–5 students.
2. Use mutual funds or bonds.
3. Visit a stock exchange.
4. Create all-class line graphs to track gains and losses of individual stocks.
5. Create pie charts that show a student's "investment portfolio," or the specific stocks purchased and percentage of overall investment.

Total Number of Shares: 180

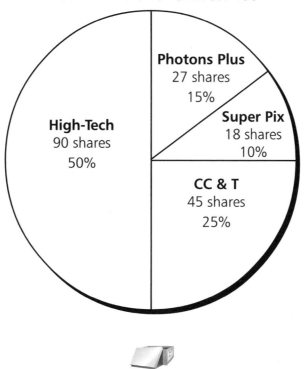

PAIRED PARTNERS

ACTIVITY-AT-A-GLANCE

Purpose

Use the problem-solving process in mathematics.

When to Use

Use throughout a lesson or unit to teach students a mathematical problem-solving process and to enable students to use the process as independent learners.

What You'll Need

❑ Step-by-step chart

What to Do

1. Randomly assign students as partners.
2. On the board or overhead, show a chart listing the steps for a tightly structured problem-solving process.
3. Walk students through each step with a sample problem. Check for understanding at each step.
4. Have students work in pairs to review the entire process, one partner serving as the questioner-recorder. Show how this role guides the other person through the process. Check for understanding.
5. Conduct a practice session. Monitor and coach the pairs. Review common difficulties with the entire class before the next round.
6. Ask for volunteers to review how they solved the problem and how the questioner helped. Use the step-by-step chart as needed.

IRI/SkyLight Training and Publishing, Inc.

7. Reverse the partners' roles and repeat the process.

8. Provide additional problems, 2 at a time, for the pairs to use.

9. Coach the class as a means of refining the process. Eventually, remove the step-by-step chart so that students work through the process without a visual guide.

Variations

1. Check for understanding as often as necessary.

2. Initially, keep the pairs together. After the students can do the process, vary the partnerships.

PROBLEM-SOLVING STRATEGIES

ACTIVITY-AT-A-GLANCE

Purpose

Become familiar with multiple problem-solving strategies.

When to Use

Each time students practice problem solving in a unit or lesson, use the Problem-Solving Strategies Wheel.

What You'll Need

❏ Problem-Solving Strategies Wheel

What to Do

1. Create a cardboard Problem-Solving Strategies Wheel prior to actual classroom usage. (See sample on next page.) Explain wheel to students.

2. Provide a mathematics problem from the textbook. Spin the spinner and ask a student to follow the instructions given on the wheel.

3. Review how the student demonstrated the technique.

4. Spin the spinner again to select another strategy to use for the same mathematics problem. Repeat until several strategies have been demonstrated.

Problem-Solving Strategies Wheel

Match your solution with the original goal. Does it make sense? Is it accurate?

Read the problem carefully. Reread if necessary.

Be flexible. Try different approaches.

Determine the meaning of key words or special terms.

Work backward from the final result.

State the goal in your own words.

Use systematic trial and error (guess and check).

List the important information.

Recall similar problems and recall how they were solved.

Draw a picture or diagram of the problem.

Break the problem into smaller pieces.

Look for patterns.

Variations

1. Use the wheel before students work on a mathematics problem and assign the selected strategy to the entire class.

2. Use the wheel *after* students have completed an assignment.

3. Use pairs to practice the techniques.

4. Provide each student with a wheel to use during homework tasks.

COACHING CARD

ACTIVITY-AT-A-GLANCE

Purpose

Use a variety of thinking skills to learn material and respond to questions.

When to Use

Use during guided practice, homework, class discussions, or when students, alone or in groups, are completing work in the classroom.

What You'll Need

❑ Coaching card

What to Do

1. Make a coaching card that lists thinking strategies and questions to elicit different levels of thinking skills. (See sample on next page.)

2. Each day, select one strategy to use to elicit student responses. Select a variety of questions based on unit content and desired level of thinking skills.

Variations

1. Provide appropriate questions on a coaching card for pairs or cooperative base groups to use during collaborative tasks.

2. Ask students to create questions for a review or test based on a specific type of thinking skill (e.g., knowledge, application, evaluation).

Coaching Card

STRATEGIES TO EXTEND STUDENT THINKING

- **Remember wait time I and II**
  Provide at least three seconds of thinking time after a question and after a response.
- **Utilize think-pair-share**
  Allow individual thinking time, discussion with a partner, and then open up for class discussion.
- **Ask follow-up questions**
  "Why? Do you agree? Can you elaborate? Tell me more. Can you give an example?"
- **Withhold judgment**
  Respond to student answers in a nonevaluative fashion.
- **Ask for summary to promote active listening**
  "Could you please summarize [John's] point?"
- **Survey the class**
  "How many people agree with the author's point of view?" (thumbs up, thumbs down).
- **Allow for student calling**
  "[Richard], will you please call on someone else to respond?"
- **Play devil's advocate**
  Require students to defend their reasoning against different points of view.
- **Ask students to unpack their thinking**
  "Describe how you arrived at your answer" (think aloud).
- **Call on students randomly**
  Avoid the pattern of only calling on students with raised hands.
- **Encourage student questioning**
  Let the students develop their own questions.
- **Cue student responses**
  "There is not a single correct answer for this question. I want to consider alternatives."

Developed by the
Maryland State Department of Education

QUESTIONING FOR QUALITY THINKING

Knowledge – *Identification and recall of information*
Who, what, when, where, how ___?
Describe_____.

Comprehension – *Organization and selection of facts and ideas*
Retell _____ in your own words.
What is the main idea of _____?

Application – *Use of facts, rules, principles*
How is ___ an example of ____?
How is ___ related to _____?
Why is ___ significant?

Analysis – *Separation of a whole into component parts*
What are the parts or features of ___?
Classify ___ according to _____.
Outline/diagram/web_____.
How does _____ compare/contrast with _____?
What evidence can you present for __?

Synthesis – *Combination of ideas to form a new whole*
What would you predict/infer from ___?
What ideas can you add to _____?
How would you create/design a new __?
What might happen if you combined __ with _____?
What solutions would you suggest for _____?

Evaluation – *Development of opinions, judgments, or decisions*
Do you agree with _____?
What do you think about _____?
What is most important _____?
Prioritize _____ according to _____.
How would you decide about _____?
What criteria would you use to assess _____?

TREASURE MAP

ACTIVITY-AT-A-GLANCE

Purpose

Use a game format, or physical activity, to complete a problem-solving task and mathematical computations.

When to Use

Use this strategy to motivate student interest by providing a series of challenging tasks to complete or to review material before a test.

What You'll Need

❏ Cardboard sets of mathematical questions or problem-solving activities
❏ Copies of a treasure map

What to Do

1. Create 4 sets of mathematical computations or problem-solving tasks. Write them on cardboard and hide cards around the room.

2. Form 4 teams of students.

3. Give each group a treasure map with clues for finding all of the cards. Once they find a card, students must perform the task or complete the mathematical computation. Successful completion can earn students points for a grade or a competitive prize for the team with the most points.

4. Set the time limit.

5. After the hunt is done, review the results.

Variations

1. Make this an individual search. Each day, hide clues for the new tasks. When an individual finds a clue or task, he or she will complete it.

2. Hide parts of a problem on different days. Over several days, have students find the pieces so they can eventually solve the entire problem.

SEQUENCE CHART

ACTIVITY-AT-A-GLANCE

Purpose

Establish a sequence of procedures for completing a mathematical task.

When to Use

Use at the beginning of a lesson to provide a visual chart of procedures or at the end of a lesson to review procedures.

What You'll Need

❑ Sample sequence chart

What to Do

1. Display a sequence chart on the board or overhead. Explain its purpose.

2. Demonstrate a sequence of procedures needed for a computational or problem-solving task. Label these on the chart.

3. Brainstorm a list of other tasks from the course curriculum that have set procedures. Assign pairs to select 1 task and create a sequence chart for it.

4. Review the procedures for using the sequence chart.

5. Before starting new tasks, outline the sequence on a chart. Post the chart.

Sequence Chart: Long Division

1. Divide

4) 1 7 2

2. Multiply

```
        4
4 ) 1 7 2
    1 6
```

3. Subtract

```
        4
4 ) 1 7 2
    1 6
     1
```

4. Bring Down

```
        4
4 ) 1 7 2
    1 6
     1 2
```

5. Divide

```
      4 3
4 ) 1 7 2
    1 6
     1 2
```

6. Multiply

```
      4 3
4 ) 1 7 2
    1 6
     1 2
     1 2
```

7. Subtract

```
      4 3
4 ) 1 7 2
    1 6
     1 2
     1 2
       0
```

Variations

1. Introduce the chart with nonmathematical, linear procedures.
2. Use paired partners to review procedures.

SPECTRUM

ACTIVITY-AT-A-GLANCE

Purpose

Use a rating spectrum to assess progress.

When to Use

Use at the beginning of a unit to show and develop a scale that can help students assess their work. During the unit, use the scale for improvement checks.

What You'll Need

❑ No materials necessary

What to Do

1. Display a 6-point spectrum on the board or overhead.
2. Explain the spectrum by relating it to a math assignment that has 10 or more practice problems. Identify the number of questions that would need to be answered correctly for each point, or indicator of success, on the rating spectrum.

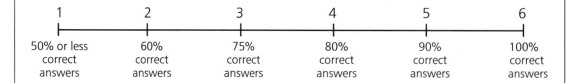

1	2	3	4	5	6
50% or less correct answers	60% correct answers	75% correct answers	80% correct answers	90% correct answers	100% correct answers

IRI/SkyLight Training and Publishing, Inc.

3. When using grades, correlate them with points on the scale (e.g., 1–2 = F; 3 = D; 4 = C; 5 = B; and 6 = A).

4. Invite students to use the scale to rate the quality of their work.

Variation

Change indicators of success based on the criteria for the lesson and the content.

THE VENN

ACTIVITY-AT-A-GLANCE

Purpose

Use a visual organizer to distinguish geometric shapes.

When to Use

Use in a unit or lesson to make comparisons that identify similarities and differences of geometric shapes.

What You'll Need

❏ No materials necessary

What to Do

1. On the board or overhead, display a Venn diagram made of 2 circles.

2. Select 2 geometric shapes (e.g., square and triangle).

3. Ask students to identify the elements and attributes each has in common, then list these in the area where the 2 circles overlap.

4. Ask students to identify the shapes' differences. List unique features of each shape in separate circles.

5. Frame a definition of each shape by stressing its unique features.

Venn Diagram

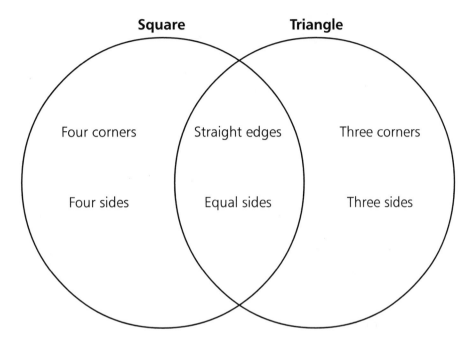

Square **Triangle**

Four corners | Straight edges | Three corners

Four sides | Equal sides | Three sides

Variation

Create Venn diagrams using numerical sets, problem types in mathematics, characters, settings, moods, or styles in literature as well as events, cultures, historic figures, philosophies, or music.

CHECK FOR UNDERSTANDING

ACTIVITY-AT-A-GLANCE

Purpose
Indicate understanding of a taught concept.

When to Use
Use throughout a lesson or unit or at the end of an explanation or set of instructions to check for student understanding.

What You'll Need
❑ No materials necessary

What to Do

1. Present information to students about how to do a new mathematical function and explain rationale.
2. Demonstrate the procedure.
3. At appropriate steps in the procedure, ask students to show understanding by indicating with thumbs up for yes, down for no, or to the side for unsure.
4. Ask students who are signaling uncertainty to tell what they *do* understand so far. Clarify as needed.
5. Ask students who don't understand to pinpoint the spots of confusion. Reteach as needed or call upon another student to coach or explain.
6. Ask students who do understand to explain the procedure to the class.

Variations

1. Give students a cue card with different colors on each side (e.g., red and green) to use instead of their thumbs.

2. Use a think-pair-share check by asking pairs to recite or summarize what was said before calling for a random check.

MATH SPORTS

ACTIVITY-AT-A-GLANCE

Purpose

Practice mathematical skills through a game format.

When to Use

Use throughout a lesson or unit to motivate students' interest in mathematics.

What You'll Need

❑ Coin
❑ Index cards

What to Do

1. Select a sport such as football, basketball, soccer, hockey or field hockey, golf, or tennis.

2. Match the rules of the game with the mathematical tasks students need to practice. If it is a team game, divide the class into teams. For example, use "addition" with football. Divide the class into 2 teams and explain the rules:

   • After a flip of the coin, team A receives the kickoff. The team's runback yardage is determined by the number of correct two-column addition problems made by the receiving team. Each correctly answered problem is worth 5 yards. A team needs 10 yards to make a "first down."

- This team gets 4 tries (4 math problems) for a first down. Teams can select a more difficult problem in an attempt to "pass the ball" for extra yardage.
- The team keeps the ball as long as it gets first downs or until it scores.

3. Have a range of easy to hard practice problems. Make sure different team members answer.

4. Have time limits for answers and the game.

Variations

1. Pick sports games that are appropriate to student interest.

2. Pick other games that use numbers such as bingo or Monopoly. Play the game but structure it so the students practice their mathematics skills.

NUMBER RUBRIC

ACTIVITY-AT-A-GLANCE

Purpose
Use a skill rubric to assess development.

When to Use
Use throughout a lesson or unit to guide students' performances against a standard or to show performance improvement.

What You'll Need
❑ Sample rubric

What to Do
1. Devise a rubric for the targeted knowledge or skill performance.
2. On the board or overhead, show students the rubric. Note how the high-end indicators can be used to show goals for improvement.
3. Each week, review the students' progress.
4. Have the final grading scale parallel the performance indicators.

49

Math Skills: Multiplication

Criteria	1	2	3	4
Accurate	Few Correct	Some Correct	Most Correct	All Correct
Process Steps Clearly Used	No Steps Shown	Missing Steps	Most Steps Correct	All Steps Correct
Work Is Checked	None Checked	Some Checked	Most Checked	All Checked

Variations

1. Change skills to be assessed.
2. Increase or decrease indicator difficulty.
3. Send rubrics home on a regular basis to communicate skill-related performance.

THE FISHBONE

ACTIVITY-AT-A-GLANCE

Purpose

Differentiate between causes and effects.

When to Use

Use throughout or at the end of a lesson to prepare students to examine important events from a cause-effect perspective.

What You'll Need

❑ Match, candle, lighter
❑ Chart paper

What to Do

1. Bring a student to the front of the classroom, light a match, and have the student blow it out. Repeat this with a candle and then with a lighter. On the board or overhead, list the student as a cause and the 3 objects as effects.

2. Ask volunteers to explain why they think the student was listed as a cause and why the objects were effects. Use questions to elicit definitions for and examples of cause and effect.

3. Explain that they are going to use a tool, the fishbone diagram, to help them understand more complex causes and effects. Display a model of the fishbone diagram. Show examples and gather ideas to fill in the blanks.

Fishbone Diagram

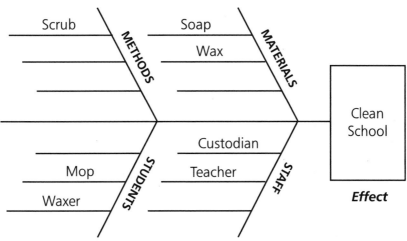

4. Create mixed-ability teams of 3–5 students. Assign roles and supply chart paper to each team. Have a recorder outline the fishbone diagram.

5. Brainstorm a list of familiar effects in the school or community. Let each group select its effect, place it on the diagram, and then build causes and examples.

6. Post the completed diagrams. Use a rotating system so that each group has the opportunity to inspect all the diagrams.

7. Brainstorm situations for which students might find this tool to be useful. Here are same examples:

   • Language arts: causes of a conflict between characters.

   • History: causes of a major historic event such as a war.

   • Science: causes of a chemical reaction.

   • Health: damage from drug use.

50

8. Select an appropriate cause-effect issue in the next unit of study. Review the fishbone diagram process before having students create the pattern. Post and carousel the pattern before discussing the unit through the perspective of cause and effect.

9. Conclude the unit lesson by assessing:

   • Individual ability to use the fishbone diagram with a new cause-effect topic.

   • Each student's understanding of the terms.

   • Students' understanding of the unit material examined through the cause-effect pattern.

Variations

1. For younger students, stay with concrete cause-effect patterns familiar to them.

2. For older students, move from the simple model to complex examples using the course content.

3. Challenge older students to explain various connections and their importance. Debate priority selections, causes, and effects.

SECTION THREE

VISUAL/ SPATIAL

HOURGLASS

 ACTIVITY-AT-A-GLANCE

Purpose

Construct "what if" questions based on prior knowledge of a topic or an idea.

When to Use

Use at the start of a new lesson, unit, or project or to bridge between subtopics.

What You'll Need

❏ Hourglass graphic

What to Do

1. Introduce the central idea or topic of the new lesson, unit, or project. Display an hourglass graphic on the board or overhead. Write the topic in the center of the image. Describe how the hourglass shape can be used as a visual organizer for recalling prior knowledge (convergent thinking) and for building "what if" questions (divergent thinking).

2. Invite the class to brainstorm what they know about the topic. Write these items in the upper portion of the hourglass. Then brainstorm "what if" questions about these ideas, and write them in the lower portion. Encourage students to combine ideas from the list to frame "what if" questions that will help them investigate the topic further. Using their list, provide examples.

Know/Recall

California condors are endangered.

So are spotted owls.

Elephants are killed for their tusks.

TOPIC
ENDANGERED ANIMALS

What If?

What if it was illegal to kill any animal?

What if animals ruled the earth, not people?

What if all the animals that ever lived still existed?

3. After the "what if" list is completed, assign 1 question to each student as a subtopic to track throughout the unit.

Variations

1. Brainstorm in cooperative groups of 3 students each.

2. Have students create "what if" questions in pairs before making the all-class list. Instruct each pair to construct several questions and select its best question for the list.

3. After listing prior knowledge, use texts or other resource materials to help construct the "what if" questions.

4. Assign cooperative pairs or trios to search out answers to one of the "what if" questions. Have students work together to prepare an all-class report.

CONCEPT CONNECTIONS

ACTIVITY-AT-A-GLANCE

Purpose

Use a concept map to connect prior knowledge on a topic.

When to Use

Use with students familiar with concept maps.

What You'll Need

❑ Chart paper

What to Do

1. On the overhead or board, identify the topic or concept students will explore in a new lesson, unit, or project. Put a key word in a circle.

2. Invite students to tell something they know about the topic. Branch that item from the circle. Invite students to give more ideas to branch from the central idea or from the other ideas.

3. After 10–12 items have formed the basis of a concept map, divide the class into cooperative groups of 5 students each. After all groups have copied the beginning portion of the map, invite them to continue the map's development on sheets of chart paper. Allow 10–20 minutes.

4. When the groups are finished, post the maps and discuss their similarities and differences.

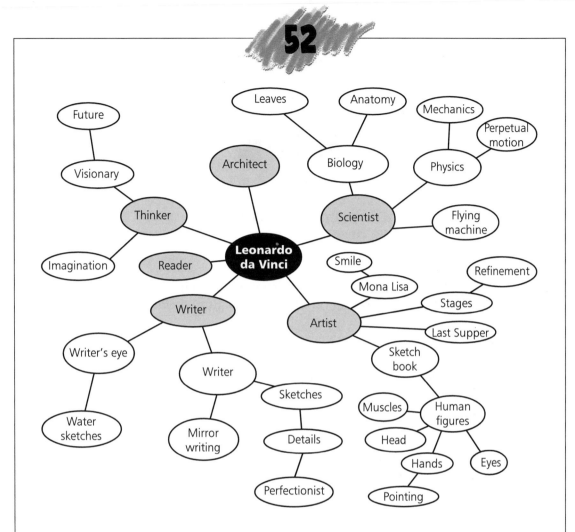

52

Variations

1. Arrange students in groups of 3–5 at the beginning of the project.

2. After students learn to use the strategy in groups, use it with individual research projects.

3. As the study of the topic continues, have groups use different colored markers to add new knowledge to the maps. This technique is especially appropriate for individual or collaborative group research inquiry projects.

KWL

ACTIVITY-AT-A-GLANCE

Purpose

Activate prior knowledge before investigating a new topic, lesson, unit, or problem. Reflect on new learning after the investigation.

When to Use

Use at the beginning of a new lesson or unit to connect prior knowledge to a new topic, to increase excitement about a new topic, or to assess learning after the completion of the lesson or unit.

What You'll Need

❑ Chart paper

What to Do

1. On a sheet of large chart paper, sketch a KWL chart. Explain or review the meaning for each letter of KWL (what we Know, what we Want to know, and what we Learned).

2. Introduce a topic and ask the class to brainstorm what they already know about it. Record the ideas in the first column of the chart. Encourage every student to give a response.

3. When the "K" column is full, repeat the brainstorming process for the "W" column. Allow thinking time between responses as necessary. Ask for clarification for meanings of terms that don't seem to fit.

53

The Planets in Our Solar System

What we Know	What we Want to know	What we Learned
Earth is one. Some have rings. Some are hot, and some are cold.	Are there any we can't see with a telescope? Could there be life on other planets?	The rings around Saturn are gases with pieces of lead. Some planets have more than one moon.

4. On the last day of the lesson, reflect on student learning by brainstorming items to list in the "L" column.

Variations

1. Invite each student (or pair) to pick an item from the "W" column. The student then becomes the expert "researcher" for that item during the lesson. He or she should report on the item when the class completes the "L" column.

2. Instead of listing "What we Want to know" in the second column, change the "W" to "P" (What we Predict we'll learn) and list the students' predictions about what they will learn.

WEB CHECK

ACTIVITY-AT-A-GLANCE

Purpose

Activate prior knowledge about a topic being introduced in a lesson or unit.

When to Use

Use at the beginning of a lesson or unit to connect or bridge students' prior knowledge to the new topic. Adjust the lesson according to what the prior knowledge check reveals.

What You'll Need

❑ No materials necessary

What to Do

1. Draw a web on the overhead, chart paper, or board. Put the topic to be introduced in the center of the web.

2. Invite students to recall what they know or have previously learned about the topic. Ask each student to provide 1 new idea. Record each new idea on a branch of the web.

3. Invite volunteers to summarize common points. Explain the connections to the lesson being introduced. Keep the web visible throughout the lesson or unit and add to it daily to keep students focused on key concepts.

IRI/SkyLight Training and Publishing, Inc.

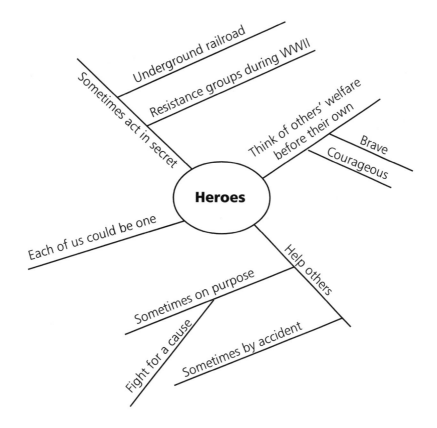

Underground railroad

Resistance groups during WWII

Sometimes act in secret

Think of others' welfare before their own

Brave

Courageous

Heroes

Each of us could be one

Help others

Sometimes on purpose

Fight for a cause

Sometimes by accident

Variations

1. Use a concept map rather than a web. Fill in what the students already know, then add new ideas.

2. Invite students to work in small groups to create their own webs.

LEARNING LINKS

ACTIVITY-AT-A-GLANCE

Purpose

Connect past experiences to new ideas.

When to Use

Use when reviewing a previous unit or when introducing a new concept to the class.

What You'll Need

- ❑ Visual aids
- ❑ 6" strips of paper
- ❑ Glue

What to Do

1. Write a word on the overhead or board that introduces the key concept or idea of a new lesson, unit, or project.

2. Use visual aids to help students understand the idea.

3. Place students in cooperative groups of 3. Ask them to think of experiences they have had with the key concept of the lesson. For example, if the concept is "respect," the students can recall times when others were respectful toward them.

4. Give each group a 6" strip of paper on which to write its example.

5. Have groups glue their strips to other groups' strips to form one chain. This shows all the links to the original concept.

Concept: Trust

Variations

1. Have group members tell about the experience and how it connects to the new idea.

2. Have each student create his or her own link in the chain and hang it across the classroom.

CREATE AN AD

ACTIVITY-AT-A-GLANCE

Purpose

Build on prior knowledge by learning more about a topic or concept.

When to Use

Use at the beginning of a new lesson, topic, unit, or semester.

What You'll Need

❏ Resource materials for the topic of study
❏ Construction paper

What to Do

1. Divide the class into cooperative groups of 3–5 students each.

2. Assemble a collection of materials that provide information on the topic of study. Instruct each group to select 4–6 resources that reflect different aspects of the topic.

3. Let the students review the materials and make 2 lists: what they know and what they want to know about the topic.

4. Ask each group to use its list to create a newspaper or magazine ad, "selling" the study of the topic.

5. Post the ads and discuss their content.

Variations

1. Use when previewing a story with primary students.
2. Use when previewing a research topic with secondary students.

WE-KNOW PARACHUTE

ACTIVITY-AT-A-GLANCE

Purpose
Build on prior knowledge while working through a unit or lesson.

When to Use
Use at the introduction of a lesson or unit to help primary and middle school students build on prior knowledge in a purposeful way.

What You'll Need
❏ Construction paper, string, scissors, glue
❏ Index cards

What to Do

1. Divide the class into pairs.
2. Have students construct a parachute using string, construction paper, and index cards.
3. Instruct students to write on each index card something they know about the lesson, unit, or topic being introduced.
4. String the parachutes across the room. As students learn something new about the topic, they may add new cards to their parachutes.

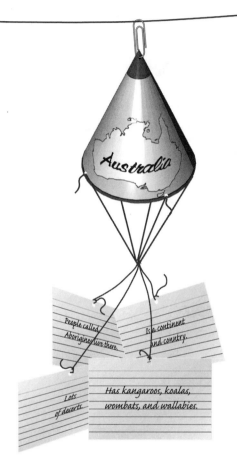

57

Variations

1. End each lesson of the unit with students adding new cards.
2. Have middle school students compete for the number of cards added each day.

MINDFUL MOBILE

ACTIVITY-AT-A-GLANCE

Purpose

Connect prior knowledge to a new topic.

When to Use

Use when introducing a new topic or unit to check prior knowledge and to prepare students for new information.

What You'll Need

❏ Wire coat hangers, string
❏ Index cards
❏ Magazines
❏ Sample mobile

What to Do

1. Make a mobile from coat hangers, index cards, string, and magazine pictures. Show it to students as a model for this task.
2. Divide the class into groups of 3 students each.
3. Instruct each group to make a mobile that illustrates what it knows about the topic to be studied.
4. Hang the mobiles and encourage students to explain them.

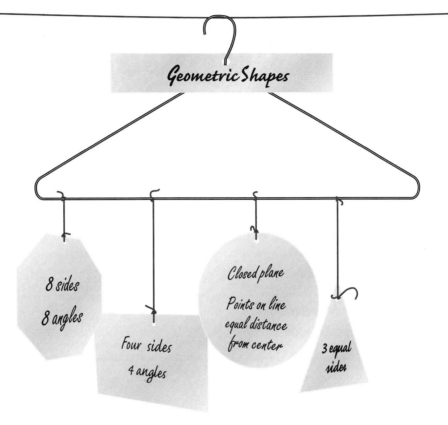

Geometric Shapes

8 sides
8 angles

Four sides
4 angles

Closed plane

Points on line
equal distance
from center

3 equal
sides

Variations

1. Let students explore the resources and text before making the mobiles.

2. Have students paste a picture on one side of an index card and record information on the other side.

3. Create mobiles by cutting out shapes of related objects (e.g., types of butterflies) and listing or sketching unique features of each.

TOPICAL MUSEUM

ACTIVITY-AT-A-GLANCE

Purpose

Make thoughtful connections between prior knowledge and a new lesson or unit.

When to Use

Use to introduce a topic as well as during a unit.

What You'll Need

❏ Various art supplies

What to Do

1. Invite students to tell what they know about museums. Discuss different types and purposes of museums.

2. Introduce the topic or concept for the lesson or unit. Form cooperative groups of 3 students each.

3. Invite each group to brainstorm a list of what its members know about the topic. Explain that each group is to select one of the statements from its list and make an artifact (e.g., sketch, sculpture, writing sample) to represent it.

4. After completing the unit of study, invite each group to make a second artifact.

5. Display the artifacts in a class museum, and have groups explain the connections between their artifacts and the topic.

Variations

1. Take students to a museum related to the topic of study before they make their first artifacts.

2. Display artifacts in a public area of the school such as a hallway or the cafeteria.

MAKE A POSTER

ACTIVITY-AT-A-GLANCE

Purpose

Express understanding of a topic through the creation of a product that expresses a clear central idea or several subideas.

When to Use

Use at the end of a unit as an assessment piece or as an opportunity for students to synthesize new information.

What You'll Need

❏ Posterboards
❏ Sample poster

What to Do

1. Have students make a poster that expresses what they learned in the lesson. Show a professional example.

2. Hang the posters in the room or hallway.

3. Randomly select 3–4 posters and ask the creators to explain the compositions.

Variation

Have students make posters about specific historical figures, time periods, literary characters and settings, cultures, mathematics concepts, science concepts, or musical figures.

MAKE A GRAPH

ACTIVITY-AT-A-GLANCE

Purpose

Make graphs to demonstrate changes in quantity.

When to Use

Use as a visual representation of quantity when integrating mathematics into other curricular areas (e.g., social studies, language arts, science).

What You'll Need

❏ Rulers, protractors

What to Do

1. Pose a question or problem related to the topic (e.g., population growth, building heights, age spans, career choices, local industry). Arrange students in pairs and instruct each pair to conduct research and gather data.

2. Select the type of graph students will use, such as a bar graph, line graph, pie chart, etc. Demonstrate an example.

3. Monitor pairs as they create their graphs.

4. Invite volunteers to show their graphs and explain the results.

Population Growth of Anytown, U.S.A.

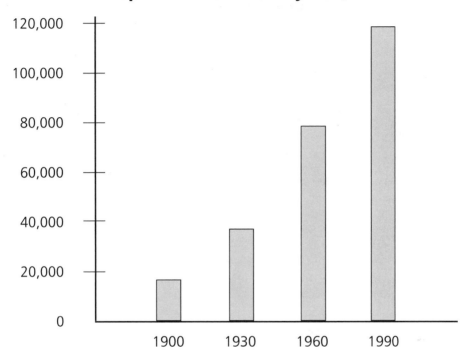

Variations

1. Assign each group to create 2 different types of graphs based on the same data.
2. Assign different questions to be researched and graphed by different pairs or groups.
3. Invite students to show their work using an overhead projector.

NONSENSICAL CREATIONS

 ACTIVITY-AT-A-GLANCE

Purpose

Synthesize disparate ideas and transfer the concept into a visual medium.

When to Use

Use to help primary students develop the ability to synthesize ideas or to help secondary students develop artistic expression and generate new ideas.

What You'll Need

❏ Drawing materials

What to Do

1. Discuss with students the meaning of the word "synthesize." Explore jobs, careers, and situations where it might be beneficial to synthesize, such as in marketing, inventing, or integrating 2 fields of knowledge.

2. Challenge students to create a synthetic name for an unusual combination, such as an alligator and a drummer or an eagle and a race car driver.

3. Ask a student to sketch a rendition of the "alli-drummer" or the "flying-racer" on the board or an overhead.

4. Have students brainstorm 2 lists, one of animals and another of people or common objects.

   IRI/SkyLight Training and Publishing, Inc.

5. Instruct students to select 1 item from each list and combine them to make nonsensical creations. The creation should have some of the characteristics from each of the original items and could have new characteristics as well. Invite students to draw their creations and to title their drawings.

6. Post the completed drawings and allow students to take turns introducing their new creations to the class.

Variations

1. Allow students to work in pairs or trios.

2. Invite students to make paintings, sculptures, or construction-paper collages of their creations.

3. Have students write stories about their creations.

DESIGN A MACHINE

ACTIVITY-AT-A-GLANCE

Purpose

Use visual/spatial intelligence to understand a concept or topic.

When to Use

Use throughout a lesson or unit to encourage students to visualize a concept, to deepen students' understanding of a concept, or to invite expression through a visual/spatial medium.

What You'll Need

❑ Samples of Leonardo da Vinci's sketches

What to Do

1. Show samples of Leonardo da Vinci's sketches. Discuss design as a medium of expression, citing examples such as architecture, consumer products, and automobiles.

2. Have each student select 1 idea from the lesson or unit and design a machine representing that idea.

3. Post the completed designs and select a way for the students to assess and/or explain their machines.

Variations

1. Form design teams to work together on the project.

2. Replace the "machine" design with an animal, vegetable, or consumer product design.

3. Require a written explanation of the finished design.

4. Form design pairs to create both a sketch and written explanation of a designed object. Collect all sketches and display them so they are visible to the entire class. Ask students to read their explanations in turn and have the class identify the corresponding sketch based on the written description.

5. Require a model of the design.

PICTURE VOCABULARY

ACTIVITY-AT-A-GLANCE

Purpose

Use visual/spatial intelligence to reinforce the meanings of vocabulary words.

When to Use

Use at the end of a unit or lesson to assure that all students know the definitions of key words.

What You'll Need

❑ No materials necessary

What to Do

1. On the overhead or board, post these 3 words: socdroop, toehole, and linebind. Explain that in the movie rendition of *Alice in Wonderland*, by Lewis Carroll, these were called "portmanteau" words, the joining of 2 or more words, as in a compartmentalized suitcase (manteau) that carries (port) more goods. Provide the definitions and ask students to draw pictures of each word. For example:

   • Socdroop—a sock that has lost its elasticity and falls down.

   • Toehole—a hole in one's sock that expands as one's toe plays with it.

   • Linebind—when there is only 1 person in front of you at a fast food restaurant, but he or she orders 25 sandwiches!

2. Ask students to invent portmanteau words and ask volunteers to sketch pictures of them on the board.

3. Discuss how pictorial images can help us remember the meanings of words.

4. Introduce 6–9 vocabulary words from a unit students are studying. For homework, have students find the definitions in the dictionary and create pictures to express each meaning.

5. Pair students. Ask them to exchange their picture definitions with their partners and to identify the corresponding vocabulary word and give a verbal definition.

6. Quiz students on the definitions of assigned words.

Variations

1. Change the difficulty of the sample words to suit the age of the students.

2. Assign students to cooperative groups and jigsaw the assigned words.

WORKING WITH VENNS

ACTIVITY-AT-A-GLANCE

Purpose
Use Venn diagrams to compare and contrast 2 or more items.

When to Use
Use to promote reading comprehension with material that calls for comparison and contrast.

What You'll Need
❑ Chart paper

What to Do

1. Review the process for using a Venn diagram.
2. Assign reading from a class textbook or other resource material. Select material that invites comparison and contrast.
3. With the class, brainstorm a list of elements of the reading assignment that could be compared and contrasted, such as 2 cultures, 2 characters, 2 settings, 2 themes, 2 situations, etc.
4. Arrange students in pairs and assign each pair a topic from the list. Instruct students to compare and contrast items within their topic and to work together to make a Venn diagram that shows what they discussed.
5. Invite pairs to present their Venns to the class.

Thomas Edison   **Orville Wright**

Invented the lightbulb and other electrical devices.

Lived 1847–1931.

Primarily worked indoors.

Famous inventor

Male

Tried some inventions several times before succeeded.

Worked with his brother.

Flew the first airplane.

Lived 1871–1948.

Lived in a tent in North Carolina.

Frequently worked outdoors.

Variations

1. Form cooperative trios and use chart paper to record information on Venn diagrams.
2. Invite students to design Venn diagrams that represent the content of a lesson.

MAPMAKING

ACTIVITY-AT-A-GLANCE

Purpose

Construct maps to organize information.

When to Use

Use in units in which location is an important element for understanding the relationship of place to place or place to event. Integrate map skills into nongeographic curricula.

What You'll Need

- ❏ Chart paper or posterboards
- ❏ Rulers, protractors
- ❏ Art supplies (e.g., paint, magic markers)

What to Do

1. Assess students' prior knowledge of maps. Highlight appropriate uses of maps, symbols, legends, etc.

2. Demonstrate to students how to make a map of 1 or more geographic locations. Provide chart paper or posterboards and other necessary art supplies based on desired sophistication of final maps.

3. Brainstorm a list of items that might be included in each map, as well as the criteria for success.

4. Arrange students in groups of 3–5 to create their maps.

5. Have each group share its completed map with the class. Instruct students to explain their maps' pluses and minuses according to the established criteria. Post completed maps in the room or hallway.

Variations

1. In primary grades, integrate this project into a study of the local community or use as a preactivity for making a community diorama.

2. In large units involving multiple locations, assign each group a different location.

CREATE A COLLAGE

ACTIVITY-AT-A-GLANCE

Purpose

Using a visual format, show the topic and subtopics in a lesson or unit.

When to Use

Use at the end of a lesson or unit to review concepts or to assess each student's understanding of key ideas.

What You'll Need

- ❏ Scissors, glue
- ❏ Posterboards
- ❏ Magazines
- ❏ Sample collages

What to Do

1. Brainstorm with the class a list of concepts students learned during the unit or lesson.
2. Introduce or review the collage format. Show samples of previous student collages or works by professional artists.
3. Present or develop with the class the criteria for a collage. Explain that the pictures represent ideas and are accompanied with a minimum of words. They form a pattern that connects ideas and may use a color scheme. Ask each student to make a collage showing the most important aspects of what he or she has learned.

4. Display completed collages. Allow each student a chance to explain his or her work in relation to the set criteria.

Variations

1. Allow students to work in cooperative pairs or trios.

2. Have students work on their collages throughout the lesson.

3. Assign the collage as a home task. Show students how to involve parents in the discussion about and creation of the collage.

MODEL BUILDING

ACTIVITY-AT-A-GLANCE

Purpose
Create a model to visually portray ideas in a lesson or unit.

When to Use
Use in lessons that lend themselves to creating models to visually portray the topic, ideas, or concepts studied.

What You'll Need
❑ Legos or building blocks
❑ Various materials for building models

What to Do
1. Check students' prior knowledge of models.
2. Use Legos or building blocks to demonstrate how to build a model. Brainstorm with the class other models students have built and the materials they used.
3. Explore ideas students could show in a model and the materials they would need to use.
4. Have students construct models to illustrate concepts or ideas related to a particular unit or topic.
5. Display the models around the classroom.

Variations

1. Use Legos or building blocks to explore patterns with primary students as they make model roadways, towers, and geometric designs.

2. Use pairs or trios to build models.

3. Invite volunteers to explain the connections between their models and the lesson or unit.

OVERHEAD REPORT

ACTIVITY-AT-A-GLANCE

Purpose

Make visual aids to accompany class reports.

When to Use

Use at the beginning of a unit or lesson to introduce students to visual aids and to prepare students to use visuals in all class presentations.

What You'll Need

❏ Overhead projector/transparencies

What to Do

1. Give students blank overhead transparencies and transparency markers.

2. Explain the criteria for creating a strong visual to use in a presentation:

   • Coordinated colors

   • Large print size

   • Three short lines of print per transparency

   • Graphics that illustrate ideas

   Illustrate good and bad examples.

3. Provide each student with a paragraph of text or a short article to read. Ask students to prepare individual reports about their reading assignments. Explain that each student is to use a transparency and create a visual that helps him or her communicate the information.

4. As students individually present their reports, highlight the positive aspects of each visual.

Variations

1. Assign pairs to make the first visual.
2. Use nontext material for the topics.
3. Assign longer presentations throughout the year.
4. Use in conjunction with a unit on charts or graphs.

STORYBOARDS

ACTIVITY-AT-A-GLANCE

Purpose

Construct a visual story line related to the content of a unit or lesson.

When to Use

Use throughout a lesson or unit to connect and sequence events or to develop students' understanding of the parts of a story (beginning, middle, end).

What You'll Need

❏ Posterboards
❏ 3 x 5 index cards
❏ Guest speaker—artist

What to Do

1. Invite an artist from an advertising agency or graphic arts company to introduce storyboards to the class.

2. Brainstorm ideas to storyboard (e.g., historic events, literature, math concepts, science procedures).

3. Instruct students to write their ideas on index cards. Limit the number of frames to be used. For example, primary students might storyboard "The Three Billy Goats Gruff" in 3 frames.

4. Ask students to assemble their index cards in sequence and attach them to posterboards.

 IRI/SkyLight Training and Publishing, Inc.

5. Hang the posterboards around the room and invite students to walk around and view them.

6. Lead an all-class discussion about the activity and the displayed storyboards.

Variations

1. Have pairs or trios create storyboards.

2. Assign the same idea or topic to everyone.

3. Have the class create storyboards for different periods in history. Post them in sequence around the room.

4. Have students create a written story or video story from the storyboards.

5. Have students create storyboards to show specific steps and their order for a sequential activity, such as lab experiments, cooking, or building projects.

71

SNAPSHOT SEQUENCE

ACTIVITY-AT-A-GLANCE

Purpose

Create pictures of key learning events in order to connect subtopics in the proper sequence.

When to Use

Use to review a lesson or to check prior knowledge before beginning a new lesson.

What You'll Need

❑ Chart paper (optional)

What to Do

1. On an overhead or chart paper, draw a blank snapshot sequence. Provide as many blanks as appropriate for the learning objectives.

2. As each step in the learning sequence is completed, invite a student to draw a picture, symbol, or sign representing the object of the lesson. Have the student explain its meaning in relation to the objective.

Variations

1. Allow each base group to keep its own snapshot chart.
2. Adjust the chart to fit the age of the students. Primary students may use a straight-line chart.
3. Have students keep a snapshot sequence in their journals.
4. Discuss the connections between and among snapshots.

72

BALLOONS

ACTIVITY-AT-A-GLANCE

Purpose

Increase understanding and encourage expression of important concepts through the creation of dialogue in a visual story.

When to Use

Use at end of a unit or lesson as a review of a topic.

What You'll Need

❏ Samples of cartoon strips
❏ Photocopies of a cartoon strip with the dialogue removed

What to Do

1. Using correction fluid, cover over the dialogue from a cartoon strip, leaving the bubbles empty. Photocopy the cartoon, making 1 copy for each student.

2. On the overhead or board, show several cartoon strip samples from a newspaper. Select age-appropriate samples. For each sample, explain the use of dialogue or thought balloons. Discuss how dialogue differs from other kinds of writing.

3. Select a topic from a unit the class has been studying. With students, brainstorm a list of problems, issues, or dilemmas related to the topic.

4. Invite each student to choose an issue and develop a point of view about it. Have students write new dialogue in the blank bubbles on their cartoon strips to express the issues and their points of view.

Variations

1. Structure pairs or trios to work on the cartoon strips.

2. Have groups of 6 share and critique completed cartoon strips.

3. Establish quality criteria and have students vote on the 3 best cartoon strips. Include these in a class newspaper.

REBUS POSTER

ACTIVITY-AT-A-GLANCE

Purpose

Synthesize reflections and transfer information to a visual form.

When to Use

Use at the end of a lesson or unit to stimulate creative thinking about the topic and to structure alternate ways of thinking about the course content.

What You'll Need

❏ Scissors, glue
❏ Magazines
❏ Posterboards

What to Do

1. With the class, brainstorm a list of important concepts learned in a lesson or unit.

2. Discuss the definition of rebus. Show a sample of a sentence that contains rebus and invite students to volunteer their own examples.

3. Arrange students in pairs, and provide scissors, glue, posterboards, and magazines. Instruct each pair to make a poster that uses words and rebus to depict what students have learned. Before they begin to work, discuss the criteria for the rebus posters. Students may draw pictures and symbols or cut them from magazines.

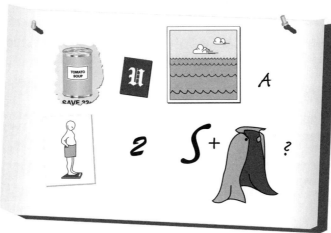

73

4. Display completed posters and invite students to view other pairs' posters. Ask students to explain why they selected the symbols they used.

Variations

1. Use the completed posters to make a quilt by arranging them on the wall in a rectangular shape.

2. Make this an individual assignment rather than a group task.

CARTOON STRIP

ACTIVITY-AT-A-GLANCE

Purpose

Evaluate the content of a lesson or unit and transfer the information to a visual medium.

When to Use

Use after students have investigated a topic or when students need to examine a topic from several points of view.

What You'll Need

❑ Sample cartoons
❑ Index cards

What to Do

1. Explain that at the end of the unit students will be evaluating all the ideas from the unit. Encourage them to keep this in mind as they work through the unit's lessons.

2. At the end of the unit, brainstorm with the class a list of key ideas reflecting what students have learned or create a matrix of topics, ideas, incidents, characters, settings, and events related to one subject area.

3. After the list or matrix is made, show a sample cartoon strip taken from a newspaper. Review the story line of the example as it is told through the pictures and the dialogue balloons. Explain that students will be creating their own cartoons.

74

4. Assign students to heterogeneous groups of 3 and have each group select 1 idea from the list or matrix to use as its cartoon's theme.

5. Provide each group with 5–7 index cards. Using the cards, each group is to depict a sequence of events related to the selected idea using both dialogue and drawings.

6. Hang the cartoon strips around the room. Allow students to walk around and view their classmates' work. Invite students to explain their work.

Variations

1. Let students work individually.

2. Ask students to create cartoons in which the characters debate the pros and cons of a particular issue. Use prior to a pro-con debate.

THE SCALE

Purpose

Determine the importance of ideas or reflect on an assignment.

When to Use

Use at the end of a lesson or unit to provide a visual image that indicates the degree to which a student has met the lesson goals. Use throughout the unit or lesson to "weigh" ideas.

What You'll Need

❏ Rubric

What to Do

1. On the board, overhead, or chart paper, sketch a bulk scale. Explain how hardware stores, grocery stores, and others use this type of scale to weigh bulk items. Check to see how many students have seen such a scale. Explain how the scale can be used as a metaphor to help students "weigh" ideas or determine the quality of their work.

2. Before starting the lesson or unit, create a rubric for students.

3. Explain each indicator on the scale; for example, outstanding (the heaviest weight), very good, acceptable, and needs improvement. Describe the point system that will be used for each indicator of success on the rubric and create a formula for translating the points to weight on the scale. Mark the generic indicators on the drawing of the scale.

4. At the end of the lesson or unit, invite students to add their points to the scale so they can weigh their performances.

Variations

1. Use with journals. Provide the rubric at the beginning of the year and establish a benchmark for the end of the year. Add additional points to the scale at key intervals during the year so students can see how improved work has a cumulative effect.

2. Have groups add the values of individual members' work to determine a group score.

SECTION FOUR

BODILY/ KINESTHETIC

BACK TO THE FUTURE

ACTIVITY-AT-A-GLANCE

Purpose

Review prior knowledge and connect to a new topic by constructing a time-travel machine.

When to Use

Use at the beginning of a course or major unit.

What You'll Need

❏ Construction paper and art materials, such as crayons, scissors, glue, toothpicks, etc.
❏ Clothesline, clothespins

What to Do

1. Arrange students into cooperative groups of 4–6 and provide them with low-cost materials for constructing a time-travel machine.

2. Let each group choose a year from the past or future.

3. Instruct students to use their textbooks and other resource materials to research information about the course content.

4. In a one-page description, have students explain how the information they learned relates to their selected year and how it could help others.

5. String a clothesline across the front of the room. Attach each group's description along the timeline.

6. Ask each group to explain why it selected the reported information.

Variations

1. Have students include in their reports what a person from the selected time period might already know about a topic related to the course content.

2. Use symbols rather than reports to represent key ideas.

PANTOMIME

ACTIVITY-AT-A-GLANCE

Purpose
Explore nonverbal expressions.

When to Use
Use at the end of a lesson or unit.

What You'll Need
❏ No materials necessary

What to Do

1. Brainstorm a list of the information, ideas, and values learned in the unit. Using an overhead or chalkboard, list these items on a triple T-chart.

2. Arrange students into heterogeneous groups. Have each group randomly select 6–8 items from the chart.

3. Instruct students to prepare a 3-minute pantomime using the selected items. The pantomime should show how each of the selected items is important to the other items and to the goals of the lesson.

4. Ask the groups to explain how the pantomime helped them assess what they learned.

Information	Ideas	Values
Louis Pasteur developed pasteurization, a preserving technique. Some molds are helpful, like those that make Blue Cheese and penicillin.	Pasteur believed bacteria caused disease. He also proved that microbes could contaminate food.	Scientists have to be persistent. People who study molds and bacteria help make a better society.

Variations

1. Arrange students in groups before brainstorming information, ideas, and values. Review the groups' charts before they begin their pantomimes.
2. For younger children, limit the pantomimes to 1 fact, idea, or value.
3. Have middle school and secondary students write a one-page essay explaining why the group selected each item in the pantomime. Collect and assess the essays.

STRETCH GOAL

ACTIVITY-AT-A-GLANCE

Purpose

Construct goals that challenge one's physical capabilities.

When to Use

Use at the beginning of a lesson, unit, course, or competitive sports game.

What You'll Need

❏ Rubber band

What to Do

1. Draw a line on a board or overhead.

2. Ask a volunteer to give a personal goal for physical fitness. Place this goal at the right end of the line.

3. Ask the student how close he or she is to the goal now. Mark this response at the left end of the line.

4. Have the student give a more ambitious, but attainable, goal. Add this "stretched" goal and lengthen the line to meet it.

5. Use a rubber band to illustrate the idea of stretching. What happens when there is no stretch? Too much stretch?

6. Pair up students. Have each share a fitness goal for the week. It should be attainable, specific, measurable, and a "stretch."

Physical Fitness Goal

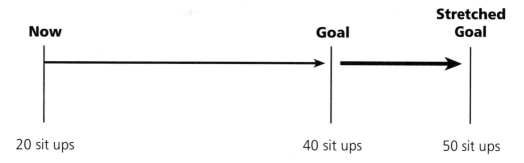

Now   **Goal**   **Stretched Goal**

20 sit ups   40 sit ups   50 sit ups

7. Allow 5 minutes for sharing. Check to see if the goals meet the criteria. Give necessary feedback.

8. At the end of a week, match pairs and have them revisit their accomplishments. Have them frame a new stretch goal.

Variations

1. Use journals or charts for students to track their improvements on a weekly basis.

2. Have students demonstrate, in pairs, the accomplishment of a stretched goal.

3. Use the process with team goals.

HIKE IT

ACTIVITY-AT-A-GLANCE

Purpose
Use walking as a form of exercise.

When to Use
Use once a week in place of an unstructured recess.

What You'll Need
❑ Suitable footwear and proper clothing

What to Do

1. Plan a walk with the class near the school. Walk the route alone first to allow proper timing.

2. Discuss and demonstrate proper walking form. Practice in a hallway or on the playground.

3. Before beginning the walk, use proper stretching and warm-up exercises.

4. Walk at a pace that challenges the slowest walker. Keep the group together—it is not a race.

5. After the walk, cool down with the students.

Variations

1. Teach the students to sing a song or march as they walk.

2. Take the students to a place where they can walk extensively (e.g., a forest preserve, park, or zoo).

3. Once a month, encourage students to make a journal entry tracking their improvements in physical well-being.

WARM-UP

Purpose

Understand the value of proper warm-up procedures before conditioning or sports activities.

When to Use

Use before all physical activity, allowing time for proper warm-up.

What You'll Need

❑ No materials necessary

What to Do

1. Ask students to identify what they know about warming up before a physical activity. After writing an all-class list on the board or overhead, ask students to identify the 5 most important warm-up tasks and explain why they are important.

2. Provide a demonstration of each warm-up activity. Follow this with a guided practice and corrective feedback.

3. Make a class bulletin board or handout. Use this to review the top 5 warm-up activities before each exercise period.

4. Before each exercise, insist that students do the warm-ups.

Variations

1. Use a coach, professional trainer, or adult athlete to demonstrate proper warm-up procedures and talk with students about the value of such procedures.

2. Invite students to work in pairs and observe and assist each other during the warm-ups.

SILLY WALK

ACTIVITY-AT-A-GLANCE

Purpose

Enjoy daily aerobic exercise.

When to Use

Use after lunch to restore students' energy or to provide a break from everyday activities.

What You'll Need

❑ A long rope

What to Do

1. Tell students that they are going to take a walk roped together. Pick the path. If the school has a gym or cafeteria, lead them on a winding walk there, especially if the outside weather is bad. If there isn't an access to a large, closed room, design the walk inside the classroom or the hallways. If there's a playground or a safe area in the school neighborhood, plan outdoor walks when the weather is suitable.

2. Line students up along a piece of rope. Encourage proper spacing as students hold on to the rope with their right hands.

3. Announce the behavior guidelines for the walk:

   • Keep one hand on the rope at all times.

   • Keep your distance from your neighbor.

   • Make only the sounds that the leader makes.

   • Copy the movements of the person in front of you.

   • Have fun. It's okay to be silly on the walk.

81

4. Take the lead. On the way, make silly sounds and motions. Each student will imitate and pass the sound or motion down the line. Keep walking, making the sounds and motions (e.g., animal sounds, car sounds, waving hands, hands on head, hops).

5. Start slowly and increase the speed of the walk and motions. On the first walk, 4–5 minutes will be okay. Add 15 seconds each day, up to 10 minutes.

Variations

1. Sing a choral song and accompany with movements during the walk (e.g., sing "Do Re Mi" and add movements).

2. Pick different locales each week.

3. Select a student leader to head up the line and make the lead movements and sounds.

SHADOW PLAY

ACTIVITY-AT-A-GLANCE

Purpose

Explore mime.

When to Use

Use with primary students when there is a need for movement and activity with a purpose.

What You'll Need

❏ Spotlight or portable plant light
❏ White sheet

What to Do

1. Set up the classroom with a strong spotlight (e.g., portable plant light). Shine the light on a light-colored wall or hang a white sheet with enough room for a student to stand between the light and the wall and cast a reflection on the wall.

2. Show students how to make finger shapes on the wall screen. Let them come up with more ideas.

3. Next, show them how to create shadows on the wall. Start with 1 student and a stationary shadow. Next, add moving shadows and groups of students who can strike shadow poses. Rather than tell the class who or what they are doing, allow the class to guess.

82

Variations

1. Invite groups of students to show shadow stories.
2. Use this activity as an introduction to the character of Peter Pan.

POSTURE PRACTICE

ACTIVITY-AT-A-GLANCE

Purpose

Demonstrate good posture.

When to Use

Use when students slouch or as an introductory physical conditioning lesson.

What You'll Need

❑ Pictures showing good posture

What to Do

1. Ask students to tell what they know about the word "posture." Add on to their ideas with additional information about the importance of standing and sitting straight.

2. Show a sketch of good standing and sitting postures. Point out what good posture looks like and demonstrate it.

3. Conduct a guided practice. Use pairs to check and coach each other. Visit among the pairs to give constructive feedback.

4. During the first week, call upon pairs several times to check postures. Do spot checks.

5. In the following weeks, make a common goal for the entire class to gain points toward a popcorn party or other reward by showing good posture during surprise checks.

83

6. Celebrate good posture by eating the popcorn only in good-posture positions.

7. Ask the class to make a list of reasons why good posture is important.

Variation

Arrange the class into mixed groups of 6–8 students. Make a competition chart and award points for observed good posture at surprise times. Each week, give a special award to the group with the highest points or to all groups that meet the criteria for success.

MONTHLY DANCERCISE

ACTIVITY-AT-A-GLANCE

Purpose

Exercise through dance.

When to Use

Use for conditioning and recreation, and structure 30 minutes a day for middle school students.

What You'll Need

❏ Music cassettes/tape player

What to Do

1. Select a dance of the month, such as a square dance, modern dance, line dance, or exercise dance.

2. Set up a tape or CD player in a large enough space for all students to participate.

3. Play the music for the easiest dance selected and demonstrate the dance steps.

4. Step-by-step, guide practice through each element of the dance. When all can do the basic moves, practice the entire dance.

5. Using a variety of music, practice the dance for a week before introducing the next version of the same dance. Continue through the month until the students can do 4 or 5 versions of the dance of the month.

Variations

1. Ask a parent or community member to teach the dances to the students.

2. Thirty minutes a day will provide the best use of this activity as a conditioning exercise, and 1–3 days a week will make it a recreational activity.

3. For primary students, teach them how to do a freeform dance in which they imagine being forces of nature (e.g., wind, storm) or animals (e.g., birds, giraffes).

4. Discuss with students the aerobic value of dancercise.

BUILD A TOWER

ACTIVITY-AT-A-GLANCE

Purpose

Enhance small motor development.

When to Use

In primary grades, use as a rainy day activity. With middle schoolers, use during an advisory period to facilitate teamwork. Use as a prebuilding activity for a subsequent model-building activity, such as building pyramids or inventions.

What You'll Need

❏ Wooden blocks, Tinkertoys, Legos, and kitchen items, such as coffee stirrers or Styrofoam cups

What to Do

1. Collect enough tower materials for all students in the class.

2. Arrange students into mixed groups of 3 and review DOVE guidelines.

3. Explain that the purpose of the task is to build the highest freestanding tower possible using the available materials within a 10-minute time period.

4. Do not model a shape. Each group will have to agree on its design and build its own tower using the available materials and all the hands in the group.

5. When the time is up, have groups sit by their models. Identify the highest freestanding tower. Head a hurrah for all the groups.

6. Ask each group to discuss the contributions of its members. Allow 3–4 minutes for this before selecting 1 member of each group to share examples. Make a list of all the contributions on the board or overhead.

Variations

1. Increase the number of blocks on successive towers.

2. Use individuals instead of groups.

3. Mix the type of materials.

4. Vary the type of model by changing the criteria (e.g., widest, longest).

PATTERN DANCES

ACTIVITY-AT-A-GLANCE

Purpose
Explore movement patterns.

When to Use
Use as a wellness unit to promote aerobic conditioning.

What You'll Need
❏ Music cassette/tape player

What to Do

1. Organize students in a circle around an open space. Tell them the lesson's purpose.
2. Count off groups of 4. Instruct each group to make a square in which students face inward but are still able to watch the demonstration.
3. Use 1 group to demonstrate each new movement pattern (the repetition of a variety of movements in an organized sequence). Start with a simple pattern to familiar music:
   • Primary grades—"Itzy Bitzy Spider"
   • Middle school—"Margarita"
4. After the demonstration, guide the practice in the groups.
5. Ask each group to invent its own pattern dance—with or without words.

6. Allow each group to teach its dance to the class. Practice each dance.

7. Hold a pattern dance festival for other classes or parents.

8. Use heterogeneous groups so that all students are included. Establish guidelines that ensure physically challenged students can perform any of the invented pattern dances.

Variations

1. Invite a professional dancer to work with the students to choreograph a pattern dance using classical or show music.

2. Integrate the pattern dance lesson with a lesson on rhyme.

PLAYGROUND RACES

ACTIVITY-AT-A-GLANCE

Purpose

Participate in cross-age races that challenge a variety of physical capabilities.

When to Use

Use in place of recess or as part of a full day of activities to promote teamwork and exercise.

What You'll Need

❑ Gold, silver, and bronze ribbons and participation certificates
❑ Materials for a variety of games

What to Do

1. Invite a class that is 3–4 years older (or younger) to join your class for this activity.
2. Arrange students into 6–8 teams. Ensure a heterogeneous balance of physical abilities on each team.
3. Set the guidelines:
   • Students should arrange themselves in pairs, 1 older and 1 younger student.
   • Only positive encouragement (cheering) is allowed.
   • All team members must participate equally.

IRI/SkyLight Training and Publishing, Inc.

4. Awards go to each finisher according to the number of teams in a race. If there are 8 teams, the top team gets 8 points and the bottom team gets 1. Each event's score will contribute to the team's total. Gold, silver, and bronze ribbons will go to the 3 top-scoring teams. All who participate receive certificates. Have the class make the awards in advance of the competition.

5. List the races:
   - Bean toss (greatest number in 2 minutes)
   - Three-legged race
   - Frisbee throw (greatest distance for throw and catch)
   - Basket shoot (greatest number in 4 minutes)
   - Club relay (fastest combined time for 4 members)
   - Wheelbarrow race
   - Water balloon toss (greatest distance until balloon breaks)
   - Push up, sit up, knee-bend relay

6. Allow teams time to practice.

7. Be sure participants understand and use safety precautions. Integrate proper warm-up and cool-down procedures.

8. Hold the competition, using parent volunteers. Follow it with an awards ceremony.

Variations

1. Add or delete events based on suitability to students (e.g., age).
2. Add an Olympic flavor with team cheers, logos, etc.

ANIMAL MATCH

ACTIVITY-AT-A-GLANCE

Purpose

Participate in an energizing activity.

When to Use

Use when students need an energizer or when it is necessary to form pairs for a task.

What You'll Need

❑ Index cards

What to Do

1. Write the names of animals on index cards (e.g., monkeys, elephants, horses, lions, wolves). Make 2 cards for each animal and make enough sets for all students in the class.

2. Assemble the class in a circle around an open area. Walk around the circle with the handful of cards and have each student select a card, which signifies a "secret" animal.

3. When all students have cards, invite them to pretend that they are a large group of animals. Each animal is looking for another of its own kind. Students are to call out animal sounds based on the animal specified on their cards and listen for a matching call of the same animal. When students find a matching animal, each pair should compare its cards to be sure the match is correct.

IRI/SkyLight Training and Publishing, Inc.

4. After all students have found their matches, ask pairs to demonstrate their calls together so the class can guess what type of animal they are.

Variations

1. Make 4 cards for each animal and have students find all the members of their group.

2. Choose animals from only 1 category, such as birds or mammals.

3. Have students create cards that can be reused for other grouping activities. Brainstorm an all-class list of animals that make sounds. Write list on overhead or board. Form student pairs and assign each pair an animal. Ask each pair to create 2 illustrated cards for its animal. Have students label their cards and write the sound the animal makes.

JUGGLE CHALLENGE

ACTIVITY-AT-A-GLANCE

Purpose
Increase hand-eye coordination.

When to Use
Use as a fun coordination task.

What You'll Need
❏ Used tennis balls or other objects to juggle

What to Do

1. Gather 36–54 used tennis balls.
2. Ask students to say what they know about juggling before explaining the purpose of this lesson.
3. Demonstrate two-ball juggling before pairing students. Have them help each other practice.
4. Allow students to advance to three-ball juggling and juggling with other objects.

Variations

1. Bring a professional juggler to class for a demonstration.
2. Hold an elimination contest to determine the most proficient classroom juggler.

IRI/SkyLight Training and Publishing, Inc.

Ideas

90

TEAM CHEERS

ACTIVITY-AT-A-GLANCE

Purpose

Develop teamwork by creating cheers that require movement.

When to Use

Use after any special team accomplishment or as a class energizer.

What You'll Need

❏ No materials necessary

What to Do

1. Form base groups and give each group the task of developing a team cheer with physical movements. The movements must fit the rhythm of the cheer.
2. Allow planning and practice time. Coach as needed.
3. Ask each team to demonstrate its cheer and use it to lead an all-class cheer.

Variations

1. Have teams construct cheers based on a specific theme or team accomplishment.
2. Hold a cheering contest for younger classes.

Ideas

ROLE-PLAY

Purpose

Use a role-playing strategy to interpret ideas, events, and skills.

When to Use

Use during a unit or lesson as a form of interpretation.

What You'll Need

❑ No materials necessary

What to Do

1. Ask students to discuss what they think the term "playing a role" means. List generated ideas.

2. Use a think-pair-share strategy to help students come up with examples of when they have played roles or of when they have experienced others doing so.

3. Explain the purpose of this lesson (to develop a learning strategy called role playing).

4. Provide a conflict situation, such as a person who is angry at another person or a leader who is trying to inspire a neighbor to help sandbag an overflowing river. Ask 2 volunteers to role play the situation.

5. Brainstorm with the class scenarios or incidents that would make good role-plays (e.g., social, historic, literary). List these on the board or overhead.

6. Divide the class into trios. Allow each group to select a topic and prepare a role-play.

7. Invite each group to perform its role-play. Have one student introduce the group's scenario.

8. After the last performance, ask the trios to list the criteria for a successful role-play. Build a class list and identify the 3–4 most important criteria.

9. Discuss the appropriate use of this strategy with the students.

Variations

1. Set a specific role-play for all groups to practice.

2. Provide scenarios.

HUMAN GRAPH

ACTIVITY-AT-A-GLANCE

Purpose

Use movement to illustrate measurements of opinion.

When to Use

Use as a physical and visual organizer to identify prior knowledge or as a midlesson check. It also can be used at the end of a unit as a knowledge assessment.

What You'll Need

❏ No materials necessary

What to Do

1. Line up students side by side in a straight line. If the room is too small, alternate which students participate.

2. Tell students they are going to make a human bar graph. The line they have formed is the baseline.

3. Provide 2 extreme positions on a topic. Designate each end of the line as representing one of the extremes. Students who agree with either of the extremes should move to the corresponding end of the line. Students who hold an "in-between" position should remain at their original locations or move closer to either end of the line to indicate their measure of agreement with a particular viewpoint.

4. Have students grouped at each location form a bar by moving into a line that is at a right angle to the baseline.

5. Test understanding with an easy choice. Instruct students who love chocolate to move to the far right and those who hate chocolate to move to the far left. More examples include:

Hate TV sports	vs.	Love TV sports
Junk food junkie	vs.	Health food nut
Early bird	vs.	Late riser
Couch potato	vs.	Exercise advocate

6. After students understand the movement, ask several students who are at different points on the graph to explain their positions.

7. Switch to serious questions about the current course topic. An example for use in a mathematics class might be:

Hands-on work	vs.	Abstract algorithms

An example for use when studying environmental issues might be:

Individual responsibility	vs.	Government regulation

Variations

1. Fit the strategy's questions to the unit or lesson content.

2. Ask the group of students at each location of the bar to discuss and then explain their position.

3. Ask a student to draw a bar graph of the "human" bar graph on the board or overhead.

CLASS REUNION NAME TAGS

ACTIVITY-AT-A-GLANCE

Purpose

Explain ideas learned in a unit.

When to Use

Use as a prior knowledge check by focusing questions on a new lesson or unit or as a check for understanding in the middle of a lesson or unit. Also, use the cards to review concepts at the end of a lesson.

What You'll Need

❏ Index cards

What to Do

1. Provide each student with a 3 x 5 index card.
2. Use a web to identify what students know about class reunions. Fill in missing information.
3. Tell students to imagine they are going to their 25th class reunion and have to prepare name tags that give specific information.
4. Use the overhead or board to identify what information is needed and how to prepare the name tag. (See example on next page.)

93

Name Tag (25 years in future)

1. Name an important idea you learned from this class or lesson.	2. Name a way this class helped you to succeed.
Name **Occupation, Business, Title**	
3. Tell about a dream fulfilled or one recalled.	4. Name an event or high point in your life.

5. After the cards are completed, instruct students to form pairs. Partners will introduce themselves using descriptions given in the center of the name tag and discuss response #1. Remind students that they are 25 years older and looking back on the past.

6. After 1 minute, ask students to remix and repeat the procedure for response #2. Repeat for responses #3 and #4.

7. Regroup as a class and ask for volunteers to share ideas about what they heard for each response.

Variations

1. Keep the questions and name tags in the present.

2. Ask specific questions for a targeted review.

3. Use the same questions at the start and end of a lesson.

4. Use as an icebreaker activity at the beginning of the school year or start of a course.

HURRAHS

ACTIVITY-AT-A-GLANCE

Purpose

Celebrate successes with classmates.

When to Use

Use to celebrate an individual, group, or all-class achievement or special contribution. Use to enable base groups to celebrate their own achievements.

What You'll Need

❏ No materials necessary

What to Do

Introduce the class to a hurrah such as the Standing "O"vation. At a signal, all students stand, clasp their hands in a circle over their heads, and say, "Oohhh."

Variations

1. The number of hurrahs is limitless. Groups can invent their own as well. Here are some silent samples:
   - Double Clam Clap (2 hands open and close like a clam)
   - Alaska Hurrah (silent shake of 2 hands overhead)
   - Yes, Yes, Yes (emphatic lip-sync statement while pulling right arm down)
   - Thumbs Up

- Whirley Bird (1 hand whirls over head like a helicopter)
- Silent Clap (hands swish by each other)
- Silent Cheer (students stand, wave hands, sit)
- Wave (silent cheer, row by row)
- Brain Wave (flutter hand by side of head)

2. Designate a student to pick the moment for a silent hurrah and lead the class in it. Use student leaders on a daily basis or for specific types of activities and rotate so that all students have the opportunity to be a hurrah leader.

FIVE CHANGES

ACTIVITY-AT-A-GLANCE

Purpose

Understand the change process.

When to Use

Use in a unit or lesson to introduce the concept of change and to identify principles of change that apply to classroom learning.

What You'll Need

❏ Journals

What to Do

1. Use a graphic organizer such as a list or web to identify students' prior knowledge of the concept of change.

2. Focus on change as a process.

3. Divide the class into pairs. Ask partners to spend 1–2 minutes studying each other. Then seat students back to back. Designate an "A" role and a "B" role for each pair.

4. Instruct "A" students to make 5 quick changes in their appearance. At the signal, each "A" will turn to student "B" and "B" will try to identify the changes.

5. Reverse roles so that "B" students make changes in their appearance and "A" students identify the changes.

6. Repeat this process with students making 5 new changes each rotation.

7. Form pairs into fours. Ask students to discuss the following questions and record their responses:

- What was easy about making the changes?
- What was difficult?
- What was learned about the change process?

Compile each group's responses in an all-class 3-column chart.

Easy	Difficult	Learned
1. Easy to guess things like one eye closed. 2. Easy to change body position. 3. Easy to use props like rubber bands.	1. Hard to identify very small changes like a bent finger. 2. Hard to think of a clever change in a hurry.	1. Some changes are obvious, others less so. 2. Changes can be big or small.

8. Ask students to formulate generalizations about change based on information in the chart. Form several hypotheses and seek consensus.

9. End with individual journal entries that complete lead-in statements such as *I learned . . .* or *I discovered . . .*

Variation

Use the chart to structure an essay on the change process.

CATCH THE DRAGON'S TAIL

ACTIVITY-AT-A-GLANCE

Purpose

Cooperate in a team competition.

When to Use

Use as a group activity during recess or a gym period.

What You'll Need

❑ Several 12-inch strips of cloth

What to Do

1. Divide the class into 2 heterogeneous teams. Explain that the teams will represent 2 dragons.

2. Allow each team to select a student to be its head and a student to be its tail. Hang a 12-inch strip of cloth from the tail's belt or pocket with at least 8 inches showing.

3. Instruct team members to stand in a row behind the head student and to place their hands on the shoulders of the person in front of them. The tails bring up the rear of each line.

4. Tell teams that the purpose of this game is for one dragon head to snare the other dragon's cloth tail while keeping its own body intact.

5. Stand the 2 dragons side by side, both facing in the same direction.

6. At a signal, one dragon is to try to capture the other's tail.

7. Remind teams that the whole dragon (entire team) must stay joined in order for them to catch the tail.

8. Be sure students understand and use safety precautions.

Variations

1. Use 3–4 teams of dragons. The champion is the team that captures the most tails.

2. Use a best-of-three format. Allow teams to discuss strategies between rounds.

INVENT A SPORT

ACTIVITY-AT-A-GLANCE

Purpose

Stimulate creative thinking processes related to sports and participate in a physical activity.

When to Use

Use to teach the critical elements of sports activities and to provide opportunities for motor-skill development.

What You'll Need

❏ Several sets of dice
❏ Equipment for chosen sport

What to Do

1. After the class has studied several different sports, create a chart in which the students identify the 5–6 elements common to all sports.

   • Brainstorm the possible elements.

   • Vote to select the top 5–6 elements.

2. Construct a chart of 5–6 columns and label each column with one of the identified elements.

3. As a class, brainstorm up to 10 specific examples of each element. For instance, if one of the elements is "having a goal," then list the types of goals used in different sports under that heading. Number each example or item. Repeat this process for each column until the chart is full.

#	Goal	Equipment	Scoring
1	(basket)	basketball	(2 points)
2	touchdown	football	6 points
3	run	(baseball and bat)	1 point

4. Use a pair of dice to roll a number for each column. If a number greater than the number of examples in a column occurs, reroll. In each column, circle the item according to the number rolled. Continue until 1 item is circled in each column.

5. Combine all of the circled items to provide the elements for a new sport. Use these elements to devise the rules, regulations, procedures, and equipment necessary for the new sport.

6. Name the sport and set up a game or tournament with the class.

7. Be sure students understand and use safety precautions.

8. Adjust the sport to include participation by all students.

Variations

1. Demonstrate the use of the chart to the class. Then arrange students in small groups and invite each group to devise a new sport.

2. Restructure the new sport (e.g., individual, noncompetitive, etc.).

3. Use the chart and dice to invent a board game.

KNOTS

ACTIVITY-AT-A-GLANCE

Purpose
Participate in a physically challenging team activity.

When to Use
Use as a fun, energizing team challenge throughout the day.

What You'll Need
❑ No materials necessary

What to Do

1. Divide students into groups of 8. (Groups must have an even number of participants.)
2. Invite students in each group to form a circle and clasp hands in the center with 2 different persons.
3. Once all hands are clasped, instruct students to unravel without letting go of anyone's hand.
4. Once a group unravels, it can encourage other groups.

Variations

1. Hold a timed competition among the teams.
2. Allow students to practice the activity and then to meet as a group to determine strategies before repeating the activity.

IRI/SkyLight Training and Publishing, Inc.

Ideas

STEP UP

ACTIVITY-AT-A-GLANCE

Purpose

Improve physical well-being.

When to Use

Use at a regular time each day to increase students' energy levels.

What You'll Need

❑ Textbooks of varying thicknesses

What to Do

1. Have students stack 2 textbooks on the floor beside their desks.

2. Explain that each day they will strengthen their heart muscles and lungs by performing a simple step exercise.

3. Demonstrate the exercise by stepping on the stacked textbooks and then stepping back on the floor. Repeat, counting each step.

4. Have students imitate the steps and counting. Start at an even pace that is easy for all to follow. After the tenth step, ask students to stand still and listen for their heartbeat and breathing rate. What do they notice?

5. Each day, repeat the process. Start slowly and pick up the pace gradually, increasing steps by one a day. Be sure to slow the pace during the last third of the activity.

Variations

1. Invite a different student each week to lead the class by counting.

2. Couple the step with other in-class exercises.

3. Add music for the count.

4. Invite a guest speaker, such as a doctor or nurse, to speak to students about the medical benefits of daily exercise.

BODY MAP

ACTIVITY-AT-A-GLANCE

Purpose

Understand the types of exercise suitable to different body parts.

When to Use

Use with primary students in place of recess or when there's a need for movement and activity.

What You'll Need

❑ Butcher paper, colored markers

What to Do

1. Create groups of 3 students each. Give each group 4-foot pieces of butcher paper (or end-of-reel unprinted newspaper) and 3 colored markers.

2. Instruct each student to lay flat on a sheet of paper and allow the other group members to trace an outline of his or her entire body. Start with the shortest student in each group and end with the tallest.

3. Instruct each child to write his or her first name over the head of his or her sketch.

4. Tell students that they are now going to name the parts of the body. On the board or overhead, write various body parts: head, eye, nose, mouth, neck, shoulder, chest, stomach, arm, hand, waist, leg, and foot.

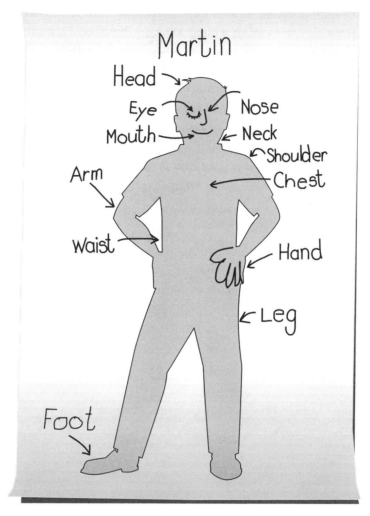

5. Point to a word on the board and sound out the pronunciation. Ask where that part is on the body maps. When there is agreement on the correct location, instruct each group to write the label in the correct spot on each member's map. Coach as needed.

6. Ask the class to identify what type of exercise might best help to strengthen these parts: neck (neck roll), arms (push ups), stomach (sit ups), and legs (running). Next to the part, have each group write the correct exercise name.

7. Hang the completed maps around the room or in the hallway.

8. Have the class sit in a clear area on the floor. Demonstrate each exercise and guide practice. Introduce only 1 exercise a week with an expanding number of repetitions.

9. Be sure students understand and use safety precautions.

10. Be sure to include warm-up and cool-down periods.

11. Five repetitions of each exercise are sufficient for early primary students. Watch that each student can do the minimum without strain. A maximum of 10 repetitions is sufficient for each exercise.

12. Avoid making exercise a competitive task.

Variations

1. Make only 1 map per group. Each group member can sign the group map.

2. Before starting the daily exercises, review the pronunciation of the body vocabulary.

3. Send the list of words home for spelling practice.

    IRI/SkyLight Training and Publishing, Inc.

SECTION FIVE

MUSICAL/
RHYTHMIC

RECALL RAP

ACTIVITY-AT-A-GLANCE

Purpose

Use prior knowledge as a lead-in to a new topic and write a rap song.

When to Use

Use at the beginning of a lesson or unit to help students connect prior knowledge with new learning.

What You'll Need

❏ Music cassettes/tape recorder

What to Do

1. Play a rap song with a narrative portion for the class. After the song, discuss the elements of rap. Tell students they are going to make a rap about the next unit of study. Share a sample and discuss the components.

2. Brainstorm what students already know about the new topic.

3. In pairs, students will use the list to create the first 2 verses and the refrain. Stop at appropriate spots to add new ideas and facts to the class list. Invite the pairs to perform their rap songs.

Variations

1. For younger students, use the list to write a nursery rhyme and teach the class to sing it.

2. Use other musical forms such as a ballad.

3. Use this strategy in the middle of a lesson to bridge subtopics.

ASSESSMENT RAP

ACTIVITY-AT-A-GLANCE

Purpose

Synthesize reflection in a musical manner.

When to Use

Use at the end of a lesson or unit to stimulate creative thinking and motivate student reflection, allowing an alternate mode of expression.

What You'll Need

❏ Music cassette/tape player

What to Do

1. Play a popular, age-appropriate rap song. Discuss how the song communicates a message.
2. Divide the class into heterogeneous groups of 3 students each, and instruct groups to brainstorm and list what they learned in the lesson. Review several of the groups' lists with the entire class.
3. Ask each group to construct a rap song based on its list.
4. Have each group perform its rap.

Variations

1. Make this an individual assignment.
2. Leave out the performances.
3. Use a different musical form that is familiar to the students.

SING A SONG TO REMEMBER

ACTIVITY-AT-A-GLANCE

Purpose

Use music as a memory tool.

When to Use

Use throughout a lesson or unit to help students memorize basic facts or components of a topic.

What You'll Need

❏ Audiotape or videotape of *The Sound of Music*
❏ Cassette player or VCR

What to Do

1. Play an audiotape or a video cut of "Do Re Mi" from *The Sound of Music*.
2. Ask students what makes the song easy to remember and what the song teaches about music (e.g., the 8-note scale).
3. Identify some other memory songs the students know, such as "Itsy, Bitsy Spider."
4. Bridge to a song that will teach students how to memorize an element of the curriculum. Teach and practice the song.

Variations

1. Use music-only tapes, and provide sheets so the class can write lyrics to the music.
2. Use tapes with both words and music.
3. Invite students to make their own "remember" songs.

POP CONNECTOR

ACTIVITY-AT-A-GLANCE

Purpose

Communicate ideas and facts through a song medium.

When to Use

Use as a lesson to teach students how to write lyrics to a song that fits a particular type of music. With students who have learned how to create a song, use this strategy at the end of a lesson or unit to provide an alternate medium to communicate ideas learned in a lesson.

What You'll Need

❏ Music cassettes/tape player

What to Do

1. Arrange students in pairs or trios.
2. Have the class name popular songs and record the list. Have pairs classify the music by grouping the songs into categories by type (e.g., rap, pop, etc.) and labeling the groups.
3. Each pair will select 1 category and list the criteria for a quality song of that type.
4. Invite each pair to select a topic to be the theme for the lyrics to a song that it will write.
5. Coach and monitor the song-writing process.
6. Have each pair present its song to the class, either by singing or playing a prerecorded tape.

7. After each performance, ask students to share the criteria they used while creating the song.

Variations

1. For primary students, use nursery rhymes as the model.
2. Use a single type of music such as rap or pop for all groups.
3. Replace popular music models with classical music or show tunes. Have the class study the selected model before having students write their own samples.
4. Use the completed songs for a parent night performance.

PLAY IT

ACTIVITY-AT-A-GLANCE

Purpose

Explore different musical instruments.

When to Use

Use in elementary and middle grades as a way to bring music into the curriculum and to create a unit that culminates in a field trip to see a concert or musical theater.

What You'll Need

❏ Pictures of musical instruments
❏ Journals
❏ Guest speakers—musicians, presentation outline

What to Do

1. Invite several local musicians to demonstrate and discuss their instruments with the class.

2. Prepare the class for the lesson and demonstration by showing pictures of the instruments and placing the pictures in a cluster with similar instruments (e.g., strings, percussion).

3. Structure the presentations by providing an outline for the presenters and the students to follow.

4. Encourage students to make a journal entry after each presentation. Have the class complete statements about each instrument, such as:

IRI/SkyLight Training and Publishing, Inc.

Name of Instrument: Accordian

Family: Reed

Origin: Vienna, Austria, in 1829

Special Features: Bellows and buttons similar to piano keys

Famous Users: Lawrence Welk, Frankie Yankovic, Myron Floren

Musical Demonstration

Questions and Answers

- *What I learned was . . .*
- *What I like about _____ is . . .*
- *What surprised me about _____ was . . .*

Variations

1. After hearing the various instruments, invite a quartet that blends instruments in different kinds of music to play for the class.

2. Identify students who play instruments. These students can make the presentations as an individual project or extra credit.

INSTRUMENT INVENTOR

ACTIVITY-AT-A-GLANCE

Purpose

Understand how musical instruments produce sound.

When to Use

Use as a unit or lesson in which students study sound as music.

What You'll Need

❑ Variety of instruments
❑ Guest speaker—musician
❑ Variety of construction materials

What to Do

1. Invite a musician to demonstrate and discuss his or her instrument.

2. After the demonstration, create an all-class list about the instrument and how it works. Use this list to develop criteria for student-created instruments.

3. Invite students to bring in materials they can use to make instruments similar to the demonstrated one. Be sure everyone contributes at least 1 item.

4. Arrange students into groups and divide the materials. Each group will make its version of the model instrument.

5. Ask each group to show its instrument and explain its features in relation to the criteria and the original instrument.

Variations

1. Start with demonstrations of different instruments from the same category (e.g., string instruments) or from several different categories (e.g., drum, violin, horn). Each group will select a different instrument to recreate.

2. Create several small bands with a mixture of instruments. Encourage each band to demonstrate a simple tune.

RHYTHMS TO RECALL

ACTIVITY-AT-A-GLANCE

Purpose

Explore a variety of musical rhythms.

When to Use

Use as part of a lesson on rhythm in poetry or songs, or as preparation for writing poetry and songs.

What You'll Need

- ❏ Music cassettes/tape player
- ❏ Coffee cans

What to Do

1. Play 3 songs for the class, each with a different rhythm (e.g., ballad, tango, and bossanova).

2. Ask students to describe the different rhythms and their importance in relation to the music.

3. Use a sonnet and ballad to show how rhythm is used to accent words in a poem or in lyrics. Contrast these with a rap song.

4. Have each student select a rhythm and mark it out with numbers (e.g., 1, 2; 1, 2; 1, 2). Tell students to indicate the strong beat by circling the stronger number.

1, ②; 1, ②; 1, ②

5. Arrange students into random groups of 5. Provide each group with an empty coffee can and invite each person, in turn, to demonstrate his or her rhythm.

Variations

1. Use pairs to create the rhythms.

2. Have each student or pair create several different rhythms.

3. After the first demonstration, pick several rhythms for a "band" of drums to play together. The creators will teach 5–6 other students how to play the rhythm in concert.

LISTENING TIME

ACTIVITY-AT-A-GLANCE

Purpose

Listen to music with a purpose or goal.

When to Use

Use with elementary students to build listening skills. Use at the start of the day, in order to initiate student focus, or after an activity period to restore student focus.

What You'll Need

❑ Music cassettes/tape player

What to Do

1. Set aside 10 minutes each day. Select a piece of music with a special feature. Study a different genre each week, such as jazz, musical comedy, or classical.

2. Introduce the musician(s) or composer(s).

3. Explain what the students should listen for: rhythm, feeling, tone, or a specific instrument.

4. Ask for concentrated silence and play the piece.

5. After the piece is completed, discuss what the students heard, felt, and thought.

IRI/SkyLight Training and Publishing, Inc.

Variations

1. After studying several different genres of music, use a T-chart or Venn diagram to compare them.

2. Study a genre of music that is connected to other topics your class is studying, such as historical periods or literature selections.

109

CONCERT TRIP

ACTIVITY-AT-A-GLANCE

Purpose
Experience a full musical concert.

When to Use
Use with middle school or secondary students. When studying a historic period, select a related concert. When studying various cultures, select related folk or classical music. When studying American literature, introduce musical comedy.

What You'll Need
❏ Music cassettes/tape player
❏ Tickets to an afternoon concert/permission slips
❏ Journals

What to Do

1. Prepare students for the trip by listening to the musical score, doing research about the composer, or reviewing the historic context.

2. Prepare students for post-concert reflection by informing them of the assessment method they will use, such as a PMI or Venn diagram, in advance.

3. After the concert, discuss the experience by asking questions that probe personal interests and personal reactions.

4. Arrange students in pairs or small groups to assess the performance. For example, ask groups to discuss the pluses, minuses, and interesting questions about the experience or to create a Venn diagram comparing the concert to a similar experience.

5. Conclude with a journal entry or invite students to complete reflective statements, such as *I liked . . .* or *I discovered . . .*

Variations

1. Select the music that fits the historical period being studied.
2. Compare folk and classical music from a given time period.

110

MUSICAL STYLES

ACTIVITY-AT-A-GLANCE

Purpose

Hear the differences between styles of soloists.

When to Use

Use when comparing and contrasting musical pieces to help students determine differences in rhythm, pitch, tenor, timbre, and other musical elements.

What You'll Need

❑ Music cassettes/tape player

What to Do

1. On the board or overhead, draw a Venn diagram and explain the purpose of the comparison.

2. Identify 2 popular singers and label each circle. Ask the class to brainstorm how each singer sounds when performing a musical piece. Enter unique characteristics in the appropriate circle and the shared characteristics in the intersection of the circles.

3. Select a sample song by each soloist. Play the songs and invite the class to list the different musical characteristics.

4. Invite the class to suggest placement of these characteristics on the Venn diagram.

Singer 1   **Singer 2**

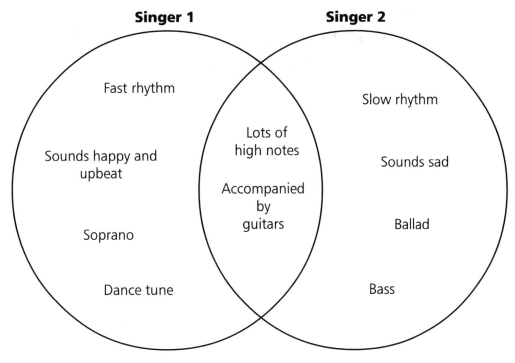

Fast rhythm

Sounds happy and upbeat

Soprano

Dance tune

Lots of high notes

Accompanied by guitars

Slow rhythm

Sounds sad

Ballad

Bass

Variations

1. Tailor the complexity of the musical selections to the background of the students. Begin with simple comparisons and popular soloists.

2. Change from popular voice soloists to classical opera singers or orchestras.

MUSICAL VOLUNTEERS

ACTIVITY-AT-A-GLANCE

Purpose

Explore interests in music by talking with professional musicians and by experiencing a variety of music.

When to Use

Use at least once every 6 weeks in the classroom.

What You'll Need

❑ Guest performer—musician

What to Do

1. Invite a professional musician to perform for the class. Ask the performer to explain each piece being performed and to discuss how his or her talent developed.

2. After the performance, encourage students to interview the musician, asking a variety of questions.

3. Make an all-class list of what students liked most.

Variations

1. Use different types of music selected for a single instrument or group of instruments.

2. Use a variety of different types of instruments.

3. Before the musician arrives, brainstorm a list of interview questions that students might want to ask.

MAGIC IN MUSIC

ACTIVITY-AT-A-GLANCE

Purpose

Share songs from films and stage productions.

When to Use

Use with middle school students to tie music to a study of poetry, rhyme and rhythm, character study, drama, or scenery design.

What You'll Need

❑ No materials necessary

What to Do

1. Ask students to recall the names of musical productions they have seen as a stage production or on television. List these on the board or overhead.

2. Form groups of 3–5 students each.

3. Allow each group to pick a production it favors and to make a web or list of the songs it remembers.

4. Have groups select a number of songs from the production that they will sing to an audience. Let the groups practice their songs. Encourage out-of-class practice and recreation of the musical scenes as they remember them.

5. Invite parents to a class production or have students perform for a primary classroom.

Variations

1. Select 1 musical production. View the film version and assign different songs to different groups of students in the class.

2. Take a field trip to see a live stage production. Before the trip, listen to a recording so students can learn the music and the melodies.

GROUP SONG

ACTIVITY-AT-A-GLANCE

Purpose

Build team cohesion through music.

When to Use

Use to build team cohesion, increase group energy, or celebrate student accomplishments.

What You'll Need

❑ Music cassette/tape player
❑ Chart paper

What to Do

1. Play a recording of the theme song for a state university or the local high school. Ask students why they think schools have theme songs (e.g., develop or increase unity and school spirit).

2. Divide the class into groups of 3 and have each group write a "spirit" song. Suggest that students use a popular song or jingle for their melody.

3. Encourage groups to use an attribute web to determine positive traits shared by group members. They can use these commonalities to write the lyrics to their songs.

4. Give groups chart paper to use to write out their lyrics.

5. Invite each group to perform its song for the class.

Variations

1. Post each group's lyrics. Have the class sing various groups' songs.
2. Use group interviews so that each group can add verses about each member.
3. Record each performance and create an audiocassette of all the songs. Accompany it with a sheet that lists the words to each song.

GROUP CHEER

ACTIVITY-AT-A-GLANCE

Purpose

Work in groups to create a rhythmic energizer.

When to Use

Use to energize the class, celebrate group accomplishments, encourage group unity before a challenging test or project, and build group unity.

What You'll Need

❏ Chart paper

What to Do

1. Move students into base groups or set up special "cheer groups" of 3 students each.

2. Ask each group to select and practice a school cheer with words and movements. Allow each group to model its cheer. Discuss the effects of cheers on the class (e.g., team spirit, energy, fun).

3. Provide groups with chart paper. Invite each group to create a cheer about its members' best characteristics. Use a matrix to identify these characteristics.

4. Have groups present their cheers to the class. Use these cheers to celebrate accomplishments throughout the year.

Our Best Features

	What is something special about this person?	What are 2 words that describe this person?	What is his or her favorite subject?
Hannah	She makes me laugh.	funny imaginative	gym
Jeremy	He always helps out.	thoughtful kind	science
Cari	She's always willing to share.	generous considerate	math

Variations

1. Tailor verses to individual or specific group accomplishments.
2. Encourage addition of cheerleading moves to each cheer.

SONG OF THE WEEK

ACTIVITY-AT-A-GLANCE

Purpose

Appreciate music as a regular part of the curriculum.

When to Use

Use to familiarize students with listening to music and assessing it against established criteria.

What You'll Need

❏ Index cards
❏ Music cassettes/tape player

What to Do

1. Ask each student to write the name of a favorite song on a 3 x 5 index card. Collect these.

2. As a class, brainstorm a list of specific criteria for the favorites. Post the list.

3. Schedule 1 song to play per week.

4. Ask students to bring recordings of their favorite songs to play for the class per the schedule.

5. Before playing a song, invite the student to use the posted criteria to explain his or her choice. Remind the class of the DOVE guidelines.

Variations

1. Have base groups vote on the "song of the month."
2. After a song is played, ask other members of the class to use the criteria to assess the song's quality.

MUSICAL REVIEW

ACTIVITY-AT-A-GLANCE

Purpose

Articulate an assessment of music based on a set of criteria for excellence.

When to Use

Use with middle school students once they understand the basic concepts of musical composition. Tie this project to the study of American history, world history, or a specific culture.

What You'll Need

❑ Chart paper
❑ Music cassettes/tape player
❑ Journals

What to Do

1. On the board or overhead, show standards for good music. Use vocabulary appropriate to the students' reading levels.

2. Develop 35 criteria of excellence. Add a Likert scale for each criterion.

Harmony

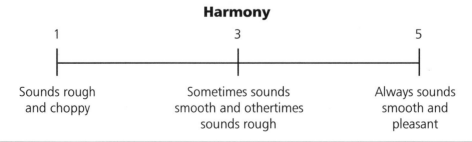

1	3	5
Sounds rough and choppy	Sometimes sounds smooth and othertimes sounds rough	Always sounds smooth and pleasant

3. Play and assess a TV jingle, popular song, and classical composition. Ask students to use the scales to evaluate each musical selection.

4. Discuss how each genre can have its own criteria. Help students adjust the criteria so they have a set for each genre.

5. Assign various musical pieces, one to a group, and ask students to apply the appropriate criteria.

6. Distribute chart paper and instruct each group to scale its assessments and prepare an explanation of its members' thinking.

7. Each group member should report on 1 criteria, but explanations must include the ideas from all the members. In addition, each group should play samples of the music for the class to hear.

8. Schedule the reports over 3 or 4 days and by genre.

9. After all reports have been presented, call for individual journal entries and invite students to share what they've written.

Variations

1. Use only 1 specific genre.

2. For advanced students, assign students individual pieces to assess.

3. As a concluding activity, compare 3 genres by constructing an all-class, triple Venn diagram.

RAP IT UP

A SUMMARIZING TASK

ACTIVITY-AT-A-GLANCE

Purpose

Use a familiar musical style as the medium for summarizing content learned in a lesson or unit.

When to Use

Use as a review, to add interest to a lesson or unit, or to create a final product in which students demonstrate their grasp of the covered material.

What You'll Need

❏ Music cassettes/tape player

What to Do

1. After concluding a lesson or unit of study, invite students, individually or in groups, to write a rap song with lyrics that summarize the ideas and facts learned.

2. Review the rap style with several examples. Students must select their own rap rhythm pattern.

3. Monitor students as they select and match ideas to the selected rhythm.

4. Review the finished products. Distribute copies to each student and invite volunteers to perform for the class.

5. After the last performance, make an all-class list that captures the important ideas and details of the finished unit.

Variations

1. Provide a single rap rhythm for all students to use.

2. Assign the rap composition as a homework task.

3. Invite parents or other classes to the performance.

4. As a final task, substitute an individual essay that communicates what was learned.

5. As a final task, provide time for an "I learned . . ." summary of the lesson or unit in student journals.

SOUNDS OF CULTURE

ACTIVITY-AT-A-GLANCE

Purpose

Explore music from many different cultures.

When to Use

Use at the end of a unit that explores different cultures in order to bring students closer to their roots and to enrich their understanding of other cultures.

What You'll Need

❑ Music cassettes/tape player
❑ World map or globe, markers

What to Do

1. Identify the cultural heritage of each student in the classroom. On a map or globe, mark the countries of origin or ancestry represented in the room.

2. Ask each student to investigate the types of music for which his or her heritage is recognized. Invite 2 students per week to share samples of music associated with their ethnic or cultural backgrounds.

3. Ask students to research and share interesting information about different cultures' musical traditions. For younger students, invite parents or other relatives to share this information. If there is a musician in the family, ask that person to play for the class.

118

Non-Western Music

Country/ Region	Instrument Used	When Used	Unique Feature
Native America (South & North)	flutes, drums, rattles	tribal rituals, religious ceremonies, social situations	5-note scale
Japan	flutes, gongs, drums, and plucked stringed instruments	theater, court festivities	no harmony
China	quin and pipa—stringed instruments	court festivities, religious ceremonies	no harmony
India	drums, tamburas, and stringed instruments such as vinas and sitars	temple and court activities	scales (called ragas) have special meanings
Africa	drums, flutes, xylophones, and stringed instruments	religious ceremonies, social rituals, festivals	complex rhythms

4. After each demonstration, discuss the unique features of the musical traditions as well as how the music is similar to (or different from) music of other cultures.

Variations

1. Make this a library assignment.

2. For younger students, take a field trip to the library's music room.

3. Create a matrix classifying musical-related topics by cultures or countries.

RHYME WORDS

ACTIVITY-AT-A-GLANCE

Purpose

Explore rhyme and write a rhyming poem.

When to Use

Use as an introduction to rhyme, as a language tool, or to help students construct memory rhymes.

What You'll Need

❏ Sample poem

What to Do

1. On the board or overhead, write "cat." Ask for a volunteer to name as many rhyming words as possible in 1 minute. Count these, and repeat the process with 2 other volunteers using the words "hot" and "roll."

2. Ask students to explain different meanings for any of the words that are homophones or homonyms. List these on the board.

3. Note that rhyming words help memory as well as provide key associations.

4. Arrange students in pairs. Have pairs write a 4–8 line poem that uses 6–12 rhymes for a single word. Share a self-created or previous student's sample.

5. Coach the pairs as they create their rhymes.

119

> The cat sat
> and watched the rat.
> The rat was chasing
> a big, fat gnat.
> The gnat flew up
> and perched on the cat.
> The rat decided
> that that was that!

6. Call for volunteers to share their completed poems.
7. Celebrate with pair-selected hurrahs.

Variations

1. Invite each student to create his or her own poem.
2. Ask students to write poems related to a theme in a lesson or unit.

NAME POEM

ACTIVITY-AT-A-GLANCE

Purpose

Write a poem based on a person's name.

When to Use

Use to review rhyming words and reflect on one's personal characteristics.

What You'll Need

❏ Sample name poem
❏ Chart paper

What to Do

1. Share a name poem with the class. Point out the use of double rhymes. (See example on the next page.)

2. Arrange students in pairs. Each person will interview the other to identify personal traits.

3. Partners will construct double-rhyme name poems about each other.

4. Post the finished poems and use a carousel (group rotation) so that all can read the finished work.

120

MATTHEW

M is for magical, an imaginative boy

A is for amiable, full of loving joy

T is for talented and smart

T is for thoughtful, with a big heart

E is for expressive, a poetic one

W is for wonderful, shining like the sun

Variations

1. Use groups of 4 or 5 students to brainstorm positive traits of each member.

2. Ask students to bring a baby photo. Attach these to the poems for a parent night display.

3. Write name poems about literary or historical figures, cartoon characters, or other imaginary or real persons.

HAIKU

ACTIVITY-AT-A-GLANCE

Purpose
Understand the haiku format and write a haiku.

When to Use
Use to introduce students to a new type of poem or writing.

What You'll Need
❑ Sample haikus

What to Do

1. On the board or overhead, share a sample haiku.
2. Discuss and list the characteristics of haiku. Use these as criteria for the students to write their own haikus.
3. Arrange students in trios, and give each group a haiku sample. Instruct each group to analyze its poem, using the criteria listed.
4. Discuss each group's analysis. Invite students to read the sample haikus and point out their qualities. After all are shared, ask students to select and discuss the haiku that best meets each characteristic.
5. Invite each student to write a haiku. Coach as needed.
6. Display the completed haikus.

121

A gently swaying
Pine tree waves good morning to
The fresh fallen snow

Variations

1. Use pairs or trios to construct the final haiku.
2. Allow individuals to analyze the sample haiku.
3. Center the haiku content around a specific unit or lesson.
4. Invite students to illustrate their haikus.

SONNETS

ACTIVITY-AT-A-GLANCE

Purpose

Appreciate the sonnet form of poetry.

When to Use

Use with advanced secondary students to emphasize the criteria of excellence for a sonnet.

What You'll Need

❑ Sample sonnets by Elizabeth Browning and other poets

What to Do

1. Ask students to identify popular songs that center on the theme of love. What do these poems say or suggest?

2. Show a sonnet sample by Elizabeth Browning.

3. Discuss with the class what it says and suggests.

4. Introduce the sonnet form used by Browning. Contrast it with those used by other famous poets.

5. Ask students to hypothesize about the effects caused by the rhyme, scheme, and meter.

6. Invite students to create 2–4 rhymed lines in one of the meters. They may want to take words from a popular love song and adjust them to sonnet form. Probe for student reactions.

7. Select 3 sonnets for students to read aloud. Allow them to practice in pairs so that they can assist each other with the use of rhyme and meter.

8. With the class, set criteria for reading the sonnets. Explain that before each reading, the student will present in writing an analysis of the rhyme and meter as well as an explanation of their contribution to the reading.

9. Give feedback based on the established criteria.

Variations

1. Encourage volunteers to write a modern sonnet.

2. Select sonnets by other poets to read and analyze.

RHYME STORIES

ACTIVITY-AT-A-GLANCE

Purpose

Write a rhyming children's story.

When to Use

Use to teach story structure and sharpen students' precise use of vocabulary.

What You'll Need

❑ Dr. Seuss stories
❑ Cardboard, construction paper

What to Do

1. Read a Dr. Seuss story to the class. Ask students to identify the common sound-alike words or rhyming patterns. What do they think the patterns add to the story? What other Dr. Seuss stories do they remember?

2. Brainstorm with the class a list of topics for a rhyming story. Choose one and create a storyboard or sequence chart.

3. Add words that emphasize a rhyming pattern.

4. Discuss with students the criteria for a rhyming story.

5. Arrange students into groups of 3 and explain that they will be working together to write a rhyming story. Each group needs to have an artist, a rhyme maker, and a storyteller.

6. Provide the materials to construct an 8–10 page, illustrated, rhyming storybook, preferably in "big book" size.

7. Invite students to read their completed stories to younger children.

8. Match each group with another and ask groups to compare the finished stories with the previously established criteria.

Variation

Invite parents to school for a story reading night.

HUMDINGER

ACTIVITY-AT-A-GLANCE

Purpose
Use music as a means to form cooperative groups.

When to Use
Use to help students with their listening skills.

What You'll Need
❑ Index cards

What to Do

1. On index cards, write the titles of familiar songs, 1 title per card. Use each song title twice so that there are 2 cards for every song. You will need 1 card per student.

2. Review all the melodies with the class, but do not reveal the titles.

3. Allow each student to pick 1 card.

4. At a signal, each student will hum his or her melody and search for the other person who is humming the same melody.

5. When all have found their partners, invite pairs to hum their melodies for the class.

6. If some students can't find their partners, ask the class to stop and be quiet and allow those students to hum alone.

Variations

1. Invite students to submit popular melodies.
2. Make 3 or 4 cards with each song's title.

SECTION SIX

INTERPERSONAL

TEAMWORK COLLAGE

ACTIVITY-AT-A-GLANCE

Purpose
Learn the individual behaviors that contribute to teamwork.

When to Use
Use when introducing students to the values of teamwork.

What You'll Need
❑ Magazines
❑ Posterboards
❑ Scissors, glue

What to Do

1. Form heterogeneous groups of 3 students each. Give each group a set of magazines, scissors, glue, and 2 sheets of posterboard. Ask each group to use the materials to make 2 collages: one showing teamwork and one showing individual performance.

2. After the groups are done, post the collages and ask volunteers from each group to explain their choices. Conclude with a discussion of the collages.

Variations

1. Use wire hangers and string to construct mobiles.
2. Make an all-class bulletin board on teamwork with a collage of cutout pictures.

OUR COMMON GOAL

ACTIVITY-AT-A-GLANCE

Purpose

Understand the importance of a common or shared goal related to teamwork.

When to Use

Use to introduce the concept of teamwork to the class or to restore team focus when cooperative groups lose focus of a common or shared goal.

What You'll Need

❑ Picture of team sports goal

What to Do

1. Show a picture of a team sports goal (e.g., soccer, football, basketball, rugby). Discuss the importance of team play and teamwork in winning a game.

2. Brainstorm a class list that shows the benefits of focusing on a common goal to gain team advantage or complete team tasks. Post the list for referral.

Variations

1. Play videotaped vignettes that show groups working together for a common purpose. Include a variety of types of groups (e.g., sports teams, marching bands, children at play). After each vignette, ask students to identify the common goal of the team or group and discuss characteristics that contributed to reaching that goal.

2. Invite a sports coach or player to talk to the class about the importance of teamwork.

3. Brainstorm a list of nonsports-related teams (e.g., orchestras, police officers, surgery team). Ask students to identify what these teams are able to accomplish or do that individuals working alone would not be able to do.

HETEROGENEOUS GROUPS

ACTIVITY-AT-A-GLANCE

Purpose

Participate in a cooperative heterogeneous group.

When to Use

Use throughout a lesson when you wish to remix students into cooperative heterogeneous groups.

What You'll Need

❑ No materials necessary

What to Do

1. Select a characteristic for grouping students (e.g., participation style) and identify 3 attributes of that characteristic (e.g., actively participates, moderately participates, needs extensive encouragement). Using observation data from the first few weeks of the school year, form a master list that identifies each student based on the selected criteria.

2. Form cooperative heterogeneous groups by selecting members with differing attributes.

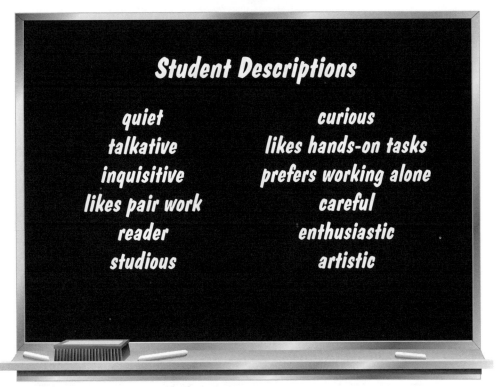

Student Descriptions

quiet	curious
talkative	likes hands-on tasks
inquisitive	prefers working alone
likes pair work	careful
reader	enthusiastic
studious	artistic

Variations

1. Form the first group from a random draw. Put each student's name in a hat and draw a whole team at one time. When a team is drawn, read students' names as a unit. After the first quarter, redraw.

2. As a class, brainstorm a list of adjectives or short phrases that describe types of students, working styles, and learning preferences. Ask students to select 3 adjectives or phrases that best describe themselves and write a short paragraph explaining their choices. Use students' self-descriptions as a tool for future grouping.

GROUP GOAL

ACTIVITY-AT-A-GLANCE

Purpose

Understand how a group goal builds teamwork.

When to Use

Use when introducing students to cooperative learning tasks, when groups are not bonding, or when groups need to reevaluate how well they are working toward a goal.

What You'll Need

❏ No materials necessary

What to Do

1. Form heterogeneous groups of 3–5 students each.
2. Discuss the concept "goal." Invite students to give examples of both individual and team goals. Guide the discussion to differentiate individual and team goals.
3. Assign a task or activity. Identify a team goal that each of the groups will pursue. After the task is complete, invite each team to assess its teamwork.
4. Brainstorm a class list of what elements, behaviors, and attitudes help teams accomplish a common goal. Conclude with a discussion of the benefits of a group goal.

IRI/SkyLight Training and Publishing, Inc.

Making Teams Work

Everyone works together.
Everyone has a turn.
People help each other.
Teach someone how to do something.
Can't be selfish.
Everyone has to participate.

Variation

Appeal to a variety of different intelligences by selecting one of the goal-directed tasks. Cooperative games, writing assignments, visual arts, and science experiments are useful when blended with "group goals."

GROUP ROUND ROBIN

ACTIVITY-AT-A-GLANCE

Purpose

Participate in group work both as an active participant and by providing other members opportunities to contribute.

When to Use

Use when 1 or 2 students are taking over a group and doing all the work, when single students are not contributing to the group work, or when it is necessary to emphasize individual accountability when contributing to the group goal.

What You'll Need

❏ No materials necessary

What to Do

1. Form groups of 3 students each. Assign a number to each student in each small group. The numbers indicate the students' sequence of response in the group.

2. Assign a task. Write on the board or overhead the questions that will guide each group's study. List 3 different questions, 1 for each group member. Each student will prepare his or her own response.

3. After all answers are prepared, ask students to share their answers in turn and to coach the other group members in turn. Reiterate the order of sharing.

4. Conclude with a discussion of the benefits and drawbacks of sharing in turn and of coaching other students to participate. Draw a T-chart on the board or overhead and list students' responses.

Sharing in Turn		Coaching Others	
Benefits	*Drawbacks*	*Benefits*	*Drawbacks*
I get a chance to talk. I get to hear everybody else's ideas.	Sometimes I want to comment on something out of turn. I plan what I'm going to say and miss hearing some things.	It's fun to encourage others. I like thinking of ways to get someone thinking in the right direction.	Frustrating when the other person doesn't care or doesn't understand. Sometimes I just want to give the answer.

Variations

1. Use an all-class "in turn" by asking a sequence of groups to share and discuss 1 question. Use the student with the corresponding number in the group to share his or her answer.

2. Ask each group to select 1 person to be the coach. Rather than members taking turns to coach, the designated coach encourages students as needed and does not answer any questions. Alternate coach assignments so that all students have the opportunity to be a coach.

3. Call for 3–5 answers on each question by moving in turn from one group to another based on a preassigned letter sequence (e.g., A, B, C).

4. Mix the sequence of questions but keep the group sequence.

GROUP LOGO

ACTIVITY-AT-A-GLANCE

Purpose
Bond with other students in a heterogeneous group.

When to Use
Use when base groups need a "bonding" boost or when students need to look at their intrinsic motivation.

What You'll Need
❑ Chart paper
❑ Sample logos

What to Do

1. Form students into their base groups and assign appropriate roles (e.g., leader, checker, encourager, recorder, reader, etc.).

2. Invite each base group to review its accomplishments and discuss what the members think are the reasons for its success.

3. Review familiar logos (e.g., Nike, Pepsi, Ford) and show samples of available logos. Discuss what the logos communicate about the companies.

4. Ask each group to create a group logo based on its "reasons for success." Provide groups with chart paper. Post the logos with accompanying signatures of group members. Invite 1 group a day to explain its logo to the class.

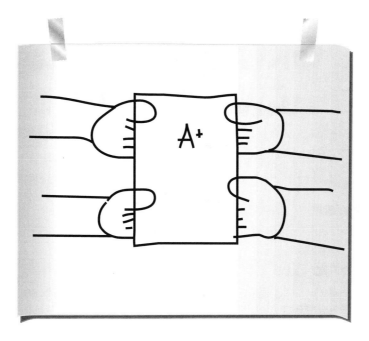

130

Variations

1. Design a class logo and display it on the door.

2. Create individual logos and ask each student to explain his or her logo to the class.

3. Ask each group to select a historic or literary figure and to design a logo that expresses that person's achievements, vision, or standards. Have students present their group's logo to the class without identifying the person it is based on and ask other groups to guess the identity behind the logo.

GROUP CHEERS AND SONGS

ACTIVITY-AT-A-GLANCE

Purpose
Bond with other students in a heterogeneous group.

When to Use
Use cheers to celebrate base group accomplishments and to energize students.

What You'll Need
❏ No materials necessary

What to Do

1. Form groups of 3 students each. Assign roles to each student in a group.
2. Explain the group goal: to create a song or cheer about the group.
3. Talk about "cheers" the students know. Elicit examples.
4. Invite each group to create a group cheer that the group will use to cheer its own accomplishments.
5. Invite each group to lead the class in its cheer.

IRI/SkyLight Training and Publishing, Inc.

131

Variations

1. After teaching a unit on poetry, assign groups to compose a poem or song about themselves or their accomplishments.

2. After completing a unit on a historic period, review popular songs from that time and have students write their own songs replicating the samples.

3. Ask groups to compose a song based on the unit's content or a specific topic by adapting or modifying the words to a contemporary popular song.

132

GROUP AD

ACTIVITY-AT-A-GLANCE

Purpose

Increase bonding among group members.

When to Use

Use when groups are starting to work and need to initiate sharing in a safe way, when groups need to improve cohesion among members, when an entire class needs to understand its shared "best attributes," or when positive communication is needed to decrease conflict in a classroom.

What You'll Need

❏ Magazines, magazine/newspaper ads
❏ Posterboards, glue

What to Do

1. Form heterogeneous groups of 3 students each and assign each member a role.

2. Identify the group goal: to create a visual advertisement about the group. Highlight that the best ads are *cohesive* representations of *shared* characteristics of the group. Discuss additional criteria so that each ad makes a powerful statement and is the group's best work. Share samples from magazines or newspapers. Distribute posterboards and magazines to each group.

3. Invite groups to use a matrix or triple Venn to identify the shared characteristics they will advertise.

IRI/SkyLight Training and Publishing, Inc.

4. Ask groups to create their ads using pictures and words cut out from magazines.

5. Display the completed and signed ads.

6. Lead an all-class assessment of the ads. Highlight those that meet the discussed criteria.

7. Instruct each group to make a list showing what each member contributed to the making of the ad. Collect lists and assess individual participation and group work.

8. Do an all-class, rotational sharing with one of the following lead-in statements: *A contribution I made is* _____ or *I am proud of myself because* _____.

Variations

1. Ask each group to use a PMI or other assessment tool to assess how well students worked together as a group.

2. Incorporate the ads into a language arts unit studying mass media.

THREE QUESTIONS
PLUS ONE

ACTIVITY-AT-A-GLANCE

Purpose

Increase participation when working in a cooperative group on a task that requires higher-level thinking.

When to Use

Use to promote individual contribution and participation within cooperative groups by requiring each group member to write an answer to every question or by providing students with specific higher-level questions that will provoke discussion.

What You'll Need

❑ Copies of articles, poems, etc.
❑ Prepared list of 3 questions related to reading material

What to Do

1. Form groups of 3–4 students each and distribute copies of a poem, short essay, short story, or newspaper editorial to each group.

2. Request that 1 student in each group reads the text aloud while the other group members listen.

3. Prepare a list of 3 questions that each student is to answer.
   • The first question will probe for the facts learned from the reading material. Preferably, ask a question that requires students to summarize the key ideas in their own words.

Story: Cinderella

1. **<u>Describe</u>** the people that lived in the household with Cinderella.

2. **<u>Tell</u>** what happened when the clock struck midnight on the night of the ball.

3. **<u>Select</u>** your favorite part of the story and explain why you liked it.

4. **<u>Explain</u>** what the author is communicating in this story.

- The second question will challenge each student to explain 1 important element of the text.
- The third question will challenge each student to tell why he or she likes or dislikes the text's ideas.

4. Ask a fourth question that requires group members to reach a consensus on the "moral" or primary message of the poem, story, or editorial.

Variations

1. Use textbook material from social studies or science as the basis of the question series.

2. Use questions that promote a specific type of thinking skill. For example, use the three-story intellect verbs to construct questions that require gathering, processing, or application skills.

JIGSAW

ACTIVITY-AT-A-GLANCE

Purpose

Use a collaborative strategy for reviewing large quantities of reading material.

When to Use

Use to check for understanding of students who most need to improve comprehension.

What You'll Need

❑ Copies of nonfictional, nonsequential material
❑ Copies of a graphic organizer

What to Do

1. Form groups of 3 students each. Provide each group with 1 copy of a nonfictional text. Be sure the material is nonsequential so that each group can read its text without reliance on a previous part.

2. Divide the text into sections based on logical breaks in the material. Assign each student 1 section of the text to read aloud while the other group members listen and take notes.

3. Provide a graphic organizer, such as the question matrix, web, target, or set of three-level questions, and ask students to list the main ideas (or other selected focus) presented in the text.

IRI/SkyLight Training and Publishing, Inc.

4. Instruct group members to share responses and information entered on their graphic organizers once the entire selection has been read and, using this information, create a single organizer that captures all of the most important information.

5. After the jigsaw is formed, conduct an all-class discussion of the material.

Variations

1. Use with a group matrix to compare biographical information on 3–5 different persons.

2. For current events, jigsaw the same event by providing different newspaper and magazine articles.

3. For secondary students, jigsaw research articles from the Internet, different points of view on a current world problem, different short stories by the same author, poems on a common topic by different poets, mathematics problems using like skills, or variations in science techniques or samples.

135

EXPERT JIGSAW

ACTIVITY-AT-A-GLANCE

Purpose

Use a collaborative strategy to review a large amount of material that requires a deep understanding of a topic.

When to Use

Use Expert Jigsaw when the class has a wide range of reading abilities and needs more checking for accuracy or when there is a large amount of material to cover.

What You'll Need

❏ Copies of nonfictional, nonsequential text
❏ Copies of a graphic organizer (e.g., web, matrix, etc.)

What to Do

1. Form groups of 3 students each. Provide each group with 1 copy of a nonfictional text. Be sure the material is nonsequential so that each group can read its text without reliance on a previous part.

2. Divide the text into sections based on logical breaks in the material. Ask students to take turns reading a section of the text while the other group members listen and take notes. Provide a specific focus, such as identifying main ideas, for the reading assignment.

3. When each group has finished its reading assignment, ask students who read the same sections to form into new groups so they can check each other for accuracy. Ask these new groups to complete graphic organizers that detail the main ideas (or other selected focus). Collect graphic organizers and check for accuracy and depth of detail.

    IRI/SkyLight Training and Publishing, Inc.

4. Return students to their original groups so that they can construct a jigsaw for the entire reading selection. Post completed jigsaw graphics and ask each group in turn to explain its graphic. Discuss any variations.

Variation

With a large amount of reading material, divide the material among the groups so that no two groups have the same material. After each group has its assignment, instruct the groups to jigsaw a graphic for the material. Provide a handout or graphic organizer so groups can select key material to share with the class. Post the graphics around the classroom and instruct each group to lead the discussion on its section of the material.

136

COACH A PARTNER

 ACTIVITY-AT-A-GLANCE

Purpose

Working in pairs, review material and coach a partner.

When to Use

Use throughout a lesson or unit, as a review of anchor material, as a way to teach a collaborative review process, or at the end as an open-book test.

What You'll Need

❑ List of questions

What to Do

1. Form pairs of students who have different levels of ability.

2. Review the goals of the unit just completed and provide each pair with a list of questions that each student will answer either orally or in writing.

3. Request that students take turns asking and answering each question. Demonstrate how students are to alternate who answers each question first.

4. After all pairs have finished the questions, check for understanding by asking a random selection of questions of the entire class.

5. Correct, clarify, or add to the responses as needed.

Variations

1. Use trios. Have the third person ask questions as the others respond and record answers in turn.

2. Assign students to compile a list of 5 questions in advance of the review. Use these student-generated questions to create the master list of questions that each pair receives for the review.

COOPERATIVE GUIDELINES

ACTIVITY-AT-A-GLANCE

Purpose

Learn guidelines for positive interaction in a cooperative group.

When to Use

Use at the start of all cooperative tasks until students demonstrate the ability to use the expected behaviors without review.

What You'll Need

❑ Sample acronym

What to Do

1. On the board or overhead, write an acronym that describes expectations for behaviors that promote positive interaction. Ask students to give examples for each letter of the acronym or to demonstrate the behavior.

2. Review the guidelines before each new cooperative task. On occasion, use an observation checklist to reinforce accountability.

Variations

1. Form base groups and ask each group to create an acronym, with accompanying phrases for each letter, to use as a team motto for positive group behavior. Create banners or posters that display the acronym and hang in highly visible areas of the room.

Primary Grade Example

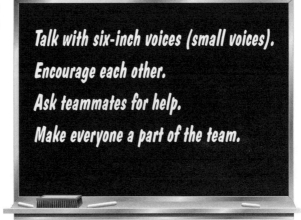

> Talk with six-inch voices (small voices).
> Encourage each other.
> Ask teammates for help.
> Make everyone a part of the team.

Middle School Example

> Watch team goal.
> Organize and plan task.
> Review individual responsibilities.
> Keep the team on task.

2. Form base groups and create an acronym to use as a team motto. Play Charades by having each base group take turns writing the acronym (letters only) on the board and acting out each letter's corresponding phrase (or initial word of phrase) while other groups guess the word or phrase.

SOCIAL SKILL T-CHART

ACTIVITY-AT-A-GLANCE

Purpose

Identify concrete behaviors that lead to development of cooperation, a social skill.

When to Use

Use once every 8–10 weeks by integrating the skill practice into a lesson.

What You'll Need

❑ No materials necessary

What to Do

1. Identify the cooperative social skill students need to develop: trust, leadership, encouragement, active listening, or teamwork. Select an age-appropriate medium such as a short story, video, role-play, or simulation in which the targeted social skill is displayed, modeled, or discarded.

2. After the students have discussed the example, show a T-chart on the overhead or chalkboard. Label the columns. Encourage students to brainstorm the behaviors that show what the skill looks like and sounds like.

Encouragement

Looks Like	Sounds Like
Smiles	Good job!
Nods	Way to go!
Thumbs up	Atta girl!

3. Post the T-chart in the room. Periodically refer to it and encourage students to practice the listed behaviors.

Variations

1. Do a triple T-chart. Add a third column, "feels like."
2. Have students create individual T-charts for different skills as the school year progresses or to reinforce a specific skill.
3. Use an observation chart to reinforce the targeted social skill.

COOPERATIVE ROLES

ACTIVITY-AT-A-GLANCE

Purpose

Demonstrate shared leadership and responsibility in a group.

When to Use

Use during a lesson or unit to teach students how to share responsibility on a team, early in the school year or a course to teach responsibilities, or as a review on a regular basis.

What You'll Need

❑ Index cards, place markers, or cardboard figures

What to Do

1. Form small groups and identify a job responsibility for each group member. Give the job an appropriate title (e.g., leader, checker, materials manager, reader, encourager, calculator, etc.).

2. Write each job title on an index card, place marker, or cardboard figure. On the back of the card, list the corresponding responsibilities. Each time a group forms, dispense the cards at random in each group and review the responsibilities. Each student should keep the card visible so job performance can be acknowledged.

Variations

1. Post students' names and their job responsibilities on a bulletin board. Assign a number to each job. Each time groups are formed, rotate job numbers or have a random number draw so students have multiple opportunities to perform each job.

2. Conduct a spot check of responsibilities during a group task by asking randomly selected students to describe their responsibilities in the group.

BASE GROUPS

ACTIVITY-AT-A-GLANCE

Purpose

Participate in a high-functioning heterogeneous group that works collaboratively over a long period of time (e.g., quarter, semester) or on an intensive multiweek project.

When to Use

Use throughout a long project or unit so students can work together in base groups, when the course of instruction calls for an extensive project, or when the planned project requires multiple talents.

What You'll Need

❏ No materials necessary

What to Do

1. Form heterogeneous groups of 3 students each. Review group guidelines and assign individual roles.
2. Select a cooperative activity familiar to the class.
3. Explain base groups.
   - What are they? (A group that will work together for ____ weeks on a certain task.)
   - Why use them? (To develop cooperative skills; to help each other on a challenging task.)

- When do we use them? (Describe the schedule when base groups will work together. For example, in a primary classroom, the base group might meet every day from 11:00 to 11:45. In the upper grades, base groups might meet every day until the project is done or on specific days such as Tuesday and Thursday.)

4. Provide a handout that describes group requirements:

- Group and individual products expected
- Instructions for project completion
- Schedule
- Criteria for success
- Assessment of group cooperation

5. In addition to checkups and scheduled class discussions *during* the project, conclude with a final assessment of how well the group worked together and met its overall objectives.

Variations

1. Change the schedule and amount of time students work together in groups.
2. Use up to 5 students per base group.
3. Intersperse task work with bonding activities.

GROUP NAME

ACTIVITY-AT-A-GLANCE

Purpose

Bond with other base group members as part of the process of forming a highly cohesive team.

When to Use

Use when groups, especially base groups, are first formed or when long-standing groups require bonding or reduction of conflict.

What You'll Need

❏ Chart paper

What to Do

1. Activate students' prior knowledge of sports teams' names. Ask for familiar examples, what the names have in common, and how they are different.

2. Form base groups. Provide chart paper to each group. Ask groups to brainstorm lists on one or more of the following topics: commonalities in the group, characteristics, and likes and dislikes of members.

3. Ask groups to review their lists, discuss similarities, and identify the strongest commonalities.

4. Invite groups to brainstorm a list of team names based on animals, natural events, or objects that represent one or more of the commonalities. Ask each group to come to a consensus on a team name that will become its base group name.

Variations

1. Ask students to brainstorm a list of familiar team names and vote within each group on the most appropriate name.

2. Supply each group with several sports magazines. Instruct groups to find team names in the magazines and vote for their favorite.

THREE-TO-ONE SYNTHESIS

ACTIVITY-AT-A-GLANCE

Purpose

Working in a small group, compose a synthesis of the group's responses.

When to Use

Use when individual accountability is an issue, to structure each student's contribution, or when students need to help each other with reading comprehension.

What You'll Need

❑ Copies of reading selection

What to Do

1. Form heterogeneous groups of 3 students each. Assign each student one of the following roles: reader, checker, or task guide.

2. Explain that this task requires students to work together as a team to create a single product. Group success is dependent on how well each individual performs his or her role.

3. Give students copies of a reading selection such as a poem, essay, short story, or section of a textbook.

4. Write the key comprehension question on the board or overhead.

5. Instruct the readers to read the material aloud softly to their groups. Instruct each group member to write a response to the posted question. In turn, students share their written answers. After all students have shared their answers, each group selects its best answer or composes a synthesis of all the answers. Task guides encourage their teammates and facilitate the group process. The checkers check that all members agree on the final answer and that each member can explain it.

6. Select several checkers at random to share and explain group responses. Discuss, clarify, and correct.

Variations

1. Give each group a set of questions so that each student will answer a different question. Vary types of questions; for example, provide a question that requires a factual response, one that requires an explanatory answer, and one that requires a hypothetical conclusion.

2. Ask each group to construct questions that can be used to review the studied material. Each group writes as many questions as there are group members, writing each question *and its answer* on a single piece of paper. Collect all the questions/answers, place in a paper bag or box, and have each student select a question. Students take turns asking questions and checking answers against the supplied answer.

143

COOPERATIVE MOBILE

ACTIVITY-AT-A-GLANCE

Purpose

Learn the distinction between cooperative, competitive, and individualistic working styles, build cooperative skills, and enhance teamwork.

When to Use

Use with middle school or secondary students to build a cooperative atmosphere in the classroom.

What You'll Need

❏ Magazines, posterboards
❏ Scissors, glue, string, and wire hangers
❏ Sample mobile
❏ Sets of 3 index cards, each set with a card that gives one of the following words and its definition: cooperative, competitive, individual

What to Do

1. Establish heterogeneous groups of 3–5 students. Assign roles and review cooperative guidelines. Explain the group activity and identify the single product each group will make. Show a sample of a completed mobile.

2. Distribute sets of index cards to each group. Using school, home, and recreational situations familiar to students, discuss the meaning of each word.

3. Distribute materials to each group: magazines, glue, string, posterboards, and a wire hanger. Invite groups to construct mobiles that show examples of cooperative, competitive, and individual activities. Hang the completed mobiles.

4. Use a small-group processing strategy to assess teamwork. Ask students how they can apply the 3 concepts they just learned to classroom activities and/or group work.

Variations

1. Construct a collage that shows examples of the 3 concepts.

2. Invite each group to enact a role-play showing each type of working style.

3. Close by listing examples of each type of working style on a triple T-chart (e.g., competitive—game show, running a race; cooperative—setting the table with a partner, having a class bake sale; individual—washing a floor, riding a bicycle).

144

FORMING GROUPS

ACTIVITY-AT-A-GLANCE

Purpose

Join a new heterogeneous group for cooperative work.

When to Use

Use any time a new heterogeneous group is needed.

What You'll Need

❏ No materials needed

What to Do

1. Determine group size. Three students per group provides a good mix of diversity and allows opportunities for each student to participate.

2. Select a grouping method:

   - **Learning modality.** Identify students' primary learning modality—kinesthetic, visual, or auditory. Form groups to include students representing each of the learning modalities.

   - **Performance.** After observing students for several weeks, rank order the class from high achievers to low achievers. Divide the list into 3 columns. Assign 1 student from each column to each group.

   - **Social skills.** Over several weeks, observe how students interact with peers and rank order the class from those who interact well to those who interact with difficulty. Make group assignments based on a mixture of students with varying social skills.

   - **Race, gender, natural origin.** Use in combination with another grouping method to create more diverse groups.

Variations

1. Identify students' strengths and demonstrated abilities based on the different multiple intelligences. Group students to provide a mixture within each group. For example, a group may include a student with high mathematical/logical ability, a student with strong visualization skills, and a student who plays a musical instrument.

2. Change task groups daily for upper grades or several times a day for primary students. This allows a constant remix that promotes classroom cohesion.

145

GROUP MOTTO

 ACTIVITY-AT-A-GLANCE

Purpose

Increase social bonding with teammates and sharing behavior when working in a group.

When to Use

Use at the beginning of a lesson or unit to initiate bonding in base groups or long-term task groups, or when conflict arises in groups.

What You'll Need

❑ Chart paper

What to Do

1. Form heterogeneous groups that will stay together for 2 or more weeks.

2. Give each group 2 sheets of chart paper. Assign roles.

3. On the overhead or board, show samples of well-known mottos such as "All for one, one for all" (Three Musketeers). Brainstorm a list of other familiar mottos.

4. Discuss with students the purpose behind mottos, or why they think individuals and teams use them. Clarify in the discussion the difference between a motto and a slogan. (Companies often use slogans, such as "You deserve a break today," as promotional devices to capture attention or present an image for advertising purposes. Such slogans differ from mottos, which are phrases that express a guiding principle or purpose.)

1. *Think up new ideas.*

2. *Come up with lots of ideas.*

3. *Try something new every day.*

5. Ask each group to create a list of positive characteristics of groups (e.g., everyone can participate, members encourage each other). From this list, invite students to select 1 characteristic as an objective to focus on during a specified period of time. Use this goal to invent their group's motto.

6. Create a poster or banner with the group's motto, inviting students to illustrate or decorate their creations and sign their names. Display posters/banners in room. As a class, discuss the benefits of creating a group motto.

Variations

1. Invite students to write a 1–2 paragraph essay describing what the motto means to them and how they intend to work toward the goal expressed in the motto. At the completion of the group work, follow up by asking students to reread their essays and write a paragraph explaining whether they met their goals and why or why not.

2. Ask students to complete lead-in statements that describe how they individually plan to support the group's motto.

146

2-4-8

 ACTIVITY-AT-A-GLANCE

Purpose

Develop a sense of community within the classroom.

When to Use

Use at the beginning of the school year to build community in the classroom, while starting to study course content, or to encourage reluctant students to join in on group work.

What You'll Need

❑ List of content-related questions

What to Do

1. Match students in mixed-ability pairs. Provide all pairs with a list of identical questions on a topic the class is studying. Be sure to vary the questions' levels of difficulty.

2. After pairs have answered every question, form quartets by joining 2 pairs. Compare the pairs' answers and compile a chart that lists the question number and shows whether the pairs agree or disagree on their answers for that question.

3. After the quartets have reviewed each question and charted their responses, pair up quartets to complete the agree-disagree chart.

4. Select several groups to report. Discuss the differences.

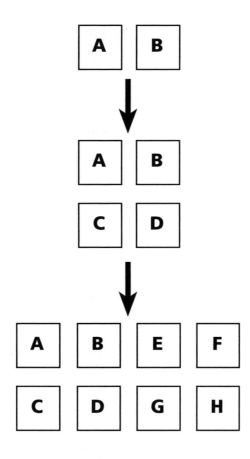

Variations

1. Select a graphic organizer to start the pair work.
2. Post the completed charts and do a carousel.

RANKINGS AND REASONS

ACTIVITY-AT-A-GLANCE

Purpose

Assess learning in a lesson or unit and share self-assessments with others.

When to Use

Use at the end of a lesson or unit so students can identify what they know on a topic and assess the importance of subtopics and ideas.

What You'll Need

❏ Chart paper (labeled and blank)

What to Do

1. At the end of a lesson or unit, post sheets of chart paper at various locations in the room (1 sheet for every 5 students). Label each sheet with one of the core ideas, goals, or outcomes of the lesson. Form groups of 5 students each and instruct each group to stand by one of the sheets, or stations. Ask groups to read the sheets and discuss what they have learned about that topic.

2. After 3 minutes of discussion, ask each group to list as many facts or ideas as possible about the topic on the chart paper (3 minutes). Rotate groups and repeat the process of discussing and listing until the sheets become full. Instruct groups that they cannot duplicate any ideas or facts listed on the sheets.

IRI/SkyLight Training and Publishing, Inc.

3. When all the sheets are filled, rotate once more and ask each group to review the information listed on the sheet and write a summary on a parallel sheet taped to the wall. Allow 10 minutes for this task.

4. As a class, discuss the summaries and call for volunteers to share their summaries. Ask all students to select what they consider the top 3 ideas, rate each idea, and be able to explain their choices. Have students share their rankings and reasons.

Variations

1. Have students work in their base groups and collectively identify the top 3 ideas.

2. After the rating discussion, ask each student to write a paper defending his or her top 3 choices.

HIGH JUMP

ACTIVITY-AT-A-GLANCE

Purpose
Identify performance standards.

When to Use
Use throughout the year to help students understand the importance of quality work.

What You'll Need
❏ No materials necessary

What to Do

1. Show a picture of a high jumper. Ask students to explain what the jumper has to do when the bar is raised or lowered. Explain how the bar stands for a standard. When a standard is raised, it is harder for more people to meet it; if it is lowered, it's easier for more people to meet it.

2. After the discussion, ask students to suggest fair standards for homework, spelling quizzes, projects, etc. Vote on these standards and develop the criteria and indicators of success for each item. Post these and use them to evaluate student work.

148

Variations

1. When developing the standards, use heterogeneous groups to develop ideas before the entire group discusses them and selects the criteria.

2. Ask students to establish standards for success for a specific group activity. Upon completion, ask students to evaluate their work against the predetermined standards.

GROUP-ASSESSMENT CARDS

ACTIVITY-AT-A-GLANCE

Purpose

Use a reusable assessment tool when working in a base group.

When to Use

Use on a regularly scheduled basis when base groups meet or with cooperative task groups at the end of tasks or projects.

What You'll Need

❏ Laminated copies of a reusable assessment tool
❏ Watercolor markers

What to Do

1. Design a group-assessment tool.

2. Laminate copies of the group-assessment tool and place them in an easily accessible location.

3. Inform groups when they are to complete a group assessment. For the first use, show students how to use watercolor markers with the laminated cards.

4. After groups have completed their assessments, collect cards and read sample responses to the class.

5. Write feedback and responses to the questions students have on the reverse side. Return these to groups for review at the start of the next class. Give general or summative feedback to the class as needed.

Group Assessment

Group Name *Magnificentos*   Date *Oct. 29*

Activity *Videotaped "A Day in My Life"*

Members	Roles
Jerome	*cameraman*
Laura	*storyboarder & creative director*
Nicky	*writer & director*
Paco	*props person & talent headhunter*
Bruce	*gofer & logistics director*

What we did well *We planned the story well—tried it out before we shot it. Also, we were very organized and had props and material ready on time.*

What we need to improve is *We should have had the actors and actresses rehearse more.*

Questions we have

1. *How many times do professional actors and actresses play a scene before the final cut?*

2. *What equipment and skills are needed to edit videotapes?*

Variation

Provide a variety of laminated group-assessment tools, such as Mrs. Potter's Questions and a PMI.

GETTING IT STRAIGHT

ACTIVITY-AT-A-GLANCE

Purpose

Understand the need to identify and clarify requirements and/or evaluation criteria for a group-based task.

When to Use

Use in the beginning of the year or course to teach students the need to clearly understand the requirements for a task and the criteria that will be used to evaluate an assignment. Use variations throughout the year to reinforce concepts as necessary.

What You'll Need

❑ Sets of Legos

What to Do

1. Form groups of 3 students each. Inform groups that they will be competing in a timed contest to build the most attractive truck, using a set of Legos. Distribute sets of Legos to each group, with instructions not to start building until you announce the start. Time groups (10–15 minutes, based on grade level). If students ask questions, tell them that the only thing you can tell them is it must be an attractive truck. Do not give any additional details. Announce the ending time, when all groups must stop work.

2. Tell groups they will get points for certain characteristics of their models. For example, trucks that used red Legos will get 10 points, trucks with yellow stripes 50 points, trucks with spare wheels 100

SCORING

Used red Legos – 10 points

Attached a horn – 25 points

Built a tower – 40 points

Created yellow stripes – 50 points

Added spare wheel – 100 points

points, etc. Write the scoring criteria on the board or overhead and ask each group to tally up its points.

3. Survey groups, asking each to show its model and give its score. Write each score on the board or overhead.

4. Congratulate the group with the highest score and ask its members to explain their "winning" strategy. Lead the class in a discussion of how chance played a part in determining the "winner" for this activity. Guide the students to the recognition that knowing established criteria and the requirements for an activity at its onset is necessary in order to work toward a specific goal.

Variation

Ask the class what would happen if you used different scoring criteria. Assign different points to each characteristic (e.g., subtract 10 points if red Legos were used) and have groups recalculate their scores. Use this as a lead-in to a discussion on determining evaluation criteria and specific instructions at the onset of activities.

SECTION SEVEN

INTRAPERSONAL

QUIET TIME

ACTIVITY-AT-A-GLANCE

Purpose

Reflect on goals and achievements on a regular basis.

When to Use

Use daily at the beginning or end of a class period to provide students a quiet time for self-reflection. May also use during any class to calm students down or during hectic, busy, or disruptive periods.

What You'll Need

❑ Journals

What to Do

1. Ask students to make a list of tasks, events, and things they do during the day, both in and out of school.

2. Write on the board or overhead: *This list makes me feel _____ because _____.* Ask students to review their lists and complete the sentence.

3. Invite students to share their completed sentences. Put DOVE guidelines in place. (Note: DOVE guidelines are used to promote a nonjudgmental, open environment for group sharing.) If students are not familiar with DOVE guidelines, introduce them:

Defer judgment

Opt for original ideas

Vast number is needed

Expand by piggybacking on others' ideas

4. Explain purpose of spending time each day to reflect. Discuss how this is helpful and why it is important. As a class, brainstorm a list of ideas for reflection such as personal goals, recent achievements, daily priorities, etc.

5. Provide several minutes for private reflection. Allow students to spend time thinking prior to writing.

Variations

1. Periodically invite students to assess "quiet time." What makes it work or why is it helpful? Is it necessary to change anything to make it more useful (e.g., spend more time, do it at a different time, resolve problems of noise or distraction)?

2. Ask students to focus on a content-related topic and to share reflections as a class. For example, use to review material at the end of a lesson or prior to a test. Ask students to list everything they know about the topic. Reflection will help students realize how well they know the material and if they need additional review.

3. Use in conjunction with conflict-resolution or peer-mediation groups to reflect on specific areas of concern. Use prior to meeting as a group to discuss these concerns.

DAILY LOG

ACTIVITY-AT-A-GLANCE

Purpose

Use writing in a daily log as a tool for reflecting on issues and concerns related to a specific class.

When to Use

Use throughout the year in any class on a scheduled basis to provide students opportunities to reflect on what they are learning and related concerns.

What You'll Need

❑ Journals or notebooks

What to Do

1. Ask each student to bring a notebook or journal to class.
2. Introduce the idea of a daily reflection log—a personal notebook in which students make periodic entries (daily, every other day, weekly) that reflect what they are learning in class, their personal goals related to the class, and difficulties or problems they encounter throughout the course.
3. Have each student label his or her log.
4. For the first entry of the year or quarter, provide one of the following lead-in statements:

- *In this class, I want to learn . . .*
- *In this class, I intend to improve . . .*
- *In this class, I hope to . . .*
- *My goal for this class is . . .*

5. Invite students to select a lead-in statement, quietly reflect on and complete it, and write their reflections in their daily logs. Allow 2–3 minutes for students to complete and date the entries.

6. For subsequent entries, offer students a lead-in or cue to encourage a specific focus. You may wish to repeat cues randomly or according to a set schedule. Possible lead-in statements follow:

- *Today (this week) in this class, I learned . . .*
- *Today (this week) in this class I improved _____ by . . .*
- *In this class, I am pleased that I . . .*
- *A difficulty I am having with this class is . . .*
- *I wish that this class . . .*

7. Collect and read students' logs periodically. Respond to students' entries with supporting comments, questions, and suggestions.

Variations

1. Students can make their own notebooks by stapling together sheets of paper with a construction paper cover or customize notebooks by decorating the cover.

2. Meet individually with students after reading their logs. Use this conference time to review students' concerns, needs, and progress.

3. Invite students to brainstorm a list of lead-in statements to use for daily writing. Post list in classroom or give copies to students to keep in their journals. Provide students the option to select their own lead-in or one that you offer the class.

TARGET

ACTIVITY-AT-A-GLANCE

Purpose

Set priorities for academic and personal challenges using a target graphic.

When to Use

Use during a project, longer-term activity, or in conjunction with an advisor-advisee or peer-mediation program when students lack focus in their thinking, have difficulty making choices, or need help in setting a new direction.

What You'll Need

❏ No materials necessary

What to Do

1. Use a think-pair-share to ask students how they decide what to do first when faced with multiple choices (e.g., study, talk on the phone, watch TV).

2. During the "share" phase, list responses on the board or overhead.

3. Explain the purpose of the "target" strategy and draw the graphic on the board or overhead.

4. Ask each student to copy the target graphic and select a "deciding" issue such as "doing homework," "getting good grades," or "participating in class."

5. Have students list 3–5 options for resolving the issue (e.g., avoid it, do it at once, do it piece by piece, do it with a friend).

Issue: Getting a Part-Time Job

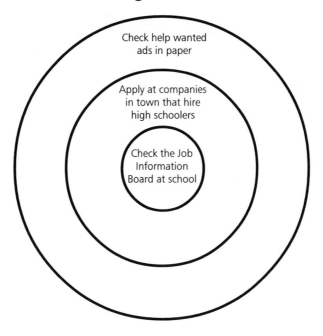

Check help wanted
ads in paper

Apply at companies
in town that hire
high schoolers

Check the Job
Information
Board at school

6. Have students put their first choice in the center of the target, second in the next ring, and third choice in the outer ring.

7. Pair up students and have them explain and defend their priorities.

8. Invite students to share their priorities and rationale with the class.

9. Build all-class lists of the:

- Benefits of a target
- Drawbacks of a target

Variations

1. Pair students with similar topics or issues.

2. Have students rearrange priorities, pair up, and discuss how this would help or hinder efforts to attain a goal.

3. Use the target strategy to examine historic or literary characters' priorities and decisions.

ONE-MINUTE MIRROR

ACTIVITY-AT-A-GLANCE

Purpose

Use a visual tool as a prompt for self-reflection.

When to Use

Use to start or end a day, class period, or advance period; as a break after a discussion or difficult task; or as a bridge between subjects.

What You'll Need

❑ Mirror
❑ Copies of One-Minute Mirror

What to Do

1. Bring a mirror to class and set it up on a wall. Activate students' prior knowledge of mirrors. Using the word "reflection," springboard into the concept of self-reflection as a way of assessing one's goals, objectives, values, successes, failures, etc.

2. Give each student a copy of the One-Minute Mirror. Explain that there are 4 variations of the mirror. Review each variation: Goals, A Concern of the Day, A Success for Today, My #1 Responsibility. Select a topic (e.g., this school year, homework, hobbies) and invite students to provide examples for each mirror, or variation.

3. Assign a new topic. Ask students to select 1 mirror and reflect for 30 seconds on that aspect of the topic. Invite students to write key words or sketch a drawing related to their reflections.

4. Each day select a different topic for the reflection.

One-Minute Mirror

Goals

1. Prepare new spelling unit.
2. Create activity cards.
3. Preview new science textbook.

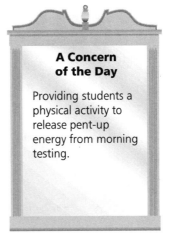

A Concern of the Day

Providing students a physical activity to release pent-up energy from morning testing.

A Success for Today

Left for school early and got new bulletin board up.

My #1 Responsibility

Getting enough sleep to fight this oncoming cold.

Variations

1. Allow each student to pick his or her reflection topic for the day.
2. Pair up students and have them discuss their reflections.
3. Extend the time and space to do the reflections. A full page in a journal is adequate once students are comfortable with the process.

SELF-PROGRESS CHART

ACTIVITY-AT-A-GLANCE

Purpose

Track progress toward goals by using a visual organizer.

When to Use

Use with primary students to introduce the concepts of setting and assessing goals. Use with middle school and secondary students to reinforce goal setting and assessment and to focus students on goals, social skills, or academic performance.

What You'll Need

❑ Copies of Self-Progress Chart

What to Do

1. Review characteristics of effective or helpful goals. Select a goal and describe each characteristic by giving examples that meet and don't meet the following criteria:
   - Important to me
   - A stretch or challenge
   - Specific and measurable
   - Possible to achieve
2. Display the Self-Progress Chart and either give each student a copy or have students copy it on paper.

IRI/SkyLight Training and Publishing, Inc.

Self-Progress Chart

Name _____Joseph Mendrick_____

Check Date _____Feb. 10_____

Goal	Progress Check	End Date
1. Complete term paper	First draft done	Feb. 28
2. Find part-time job	Applied at grocery store	March 30
3. Learn stain glassing	Signed up for class	May 30

3. Invite students to complete columns 1 and 3 by listing 3 goals and setting a date to complete each goal. Students leave the Progress Check column blank, as it will be this column that they focus on as they check their progress against their goals on a daily or regularly scheduled basis.

4. Each day (or per schedule), allow 2–3 minutes for students to check progress. Invite them to complete the Progress Check column by showing steps they have taken to achieve each goal and their outcomes.

5. At the end of the week, pair students to discuss their progress, assess where they are at, and revise goals as needed (5–7 minutes).

Variations

1. Use a single goal per week. Revise the chart so that column 1 lists individual steps to take to complete the goal.

2. Invite students to enter the charts in their journals.

3. Once a week, use a lead-in statement such as *I'm pleased that I . . .* in reference to their goal progress. Invite students to complete the statement and enter responses in journals or discuss in pairs.

4. Use the chart to identify and track goals when working in a cooperative group or as a team.

ROUND ROBIN

ACTIVITY-AT-A-GLANCE

Purpose

Complete a cooperative group task by participating in a responsible manner.

When to Use

Use to teach and reinforce shared responsibility in a cooperative group.

What You'll Need

❏ No materials necessary

What to Do

1. Form groups of 3–5 students each. Identify the task with its common goal.

2. Assign each student an equal task (e.g., complete 1 word problem and prepare to explain the answer, answer 2 chapter questions). After each has finished his or her assignment, instruct students to share the results of their task using a round-robin structure.

3. If disagreements arise, instruct the conflicting members to use a conflict-resolution strategy.

4. Monitor the groups at work to ensure correct answers and positive group behavior.

5. Check for understanding and accuracy.

6. Discuss with the class the effects of the round-robin structure.

 IRI/SkyLight Training and Publishing, Inc.

Variation

On a larger task, assign each group a topic or task in a jigsaw. Use a round-robin structure for reporting to the class.

PLUS/MINUS/ INTERESTING (PMI)

ACTIVITY-AT-A-GLANCE

Purpose

Use a graphic tool to assess attitudes, academic performance, social skills, and behavior.

When to Use

Use on a regularly scheduled basis, such as at the end of the day for primary students or end of the week for middle school or secondary students, at the completion of a major individual or cooperative group project, or at the end of a completed task such as an essay or story, lab report, test, etc.

What You'll Need

❑ PMI chart

What to Do

1. Show students the PMI chart and explain the headings: P+ (Pluses), M- (Minuses), and I? (Interesting Questions).

2. Select a topic familiar to the students such as "attending (school name)." As a class, brainstorm lists or use a round-robin structure to complete each column. Do 1 column at a time. After all 3 columns are filled, select 2 or 3 ideas for class discussion.

Topic: Sharing my first draft—When My Dog Died—with a group

P+ **Pluses**	1) Neat how some people said they liked it. 2) Got a great idea how to change the ending.
M– **Minuses**	1) One person was way too critical. 2) Kind of hard to talk about.
I? **Interesting** **Questions**	1) Would it improve my essay if I included other people's experiences of losing a pet? 2) Do I want to include more about my feelings?

Variations

1. Assess class projects such as field trips, class speakers, or major projects.
2. Assign PMI reflection for journal writing.
3. Assess affective responses to lessons that introduce new concepts or learning strategies.

MY GOALS

ACTIVITY-AT-A-GLANCE

Purpose

Establish the habit of setting and assessing personal goals.

When to Use

Use throughout a lesson or unit to focus students on final goals and achieving those goals.

What You'll Need

❏ No materials necessary

What to Do

1. Brainstorm with the class sports that use the word "goal." List the responses on the board or an overhead in a column.

2. Brainstorm areas of life (e.g., work, hobbies, sports) for which students can have goals. List these in a second column.

3. Invite students to explain how column 1 and column 2 are alike. List responses in a third column.

4. Ask each student to select 1 goal area from column 2 and write out a personal goal for that area. Give an example.

5. Ask students to review and modify the goal according to the "ABC" criteria:

   • Is it Achievable? (Is it specific enough that the student can tell steps to success?)

   • Is it Believable? (Can the student list and describe the talents he or she has that will help?)

- Is it Controllable? (Is it a goal for which the student needs only to depend on self?)

6. Pair up students. Each student will explain his or her goal and tell how it matches the ABC criteria.

7. After the pair review, invite each student to write a paragraph that:
   - Summarizes the goal.
   - Details steps to be taken to achieve goal.
   - Identifies ways to increase achievement of goal.
   - Identifies benefits for achieving the goal.
   - Modifies the goal.

Variations

1. For primary and intermediate students, make step 7 an oral activity.
2. Preselect the topic area (e.g., sports, homework assignments) that all students will use.

SELF-TALK

ACTIVITY-AT-A-GLANCE

Purpose

Use self-talk as a means to reflect on goals, aspirations, abilities, and performance.

When to Use

Use throughout a lesson or unit to teach students a simple reflection technique and to help students self-review at key spots during the school year.

What You'll Need

❑ No materials necessary

What to Do

1. Ask students, "What do you think if you hear someone talking to him- or herself?" and "Why do you think so?" Ask students if they ever talk to themselves.

2. Point out that self-talk doesn't have to be public. Every time a student thinks, he or she is talking to him- or herself. This quiet self-talk doesn't need to be heard by anyone but the person who is thinking.

3. List the following categories on the board or overhead: Goals, Aspirations, Abilities, and Performance. Select a category and give an example of positive self-talk. Following are sample responses:

   • Goals: "This week I want to visit my grandparents. What do I need to do to get ready for the trip? Let me see. I need to . . ."

- Aspirations: "Someday, I want to be a doctor in a Third World country. Why do I want to do that? I guess because . . ."
- Abilities: "It's time to think about high school. What courses do I want to take? If I want to be a salesperson, what will I need to know? I know I'm a good talker. I can convince my friends to do anything. I'm also great at math. . . ."
- Performance: "How have I done this week? Well, I completed all my homework. I did a really great job on the social studies test. I think it helped that I . . ."

4. Invite students to select a category and engage in self-talk, or have a private conversation with themselves. Allow 2–3 minutes.

5. Invite students to share with the class what they "talked" about. Ask students for feedback on the experience. For example, Was it easy to do? Hard? Was it beneficial? When would it be good to practice self-talk?

6. Summarize by identifying and describing the characteristics of self-talk:
   - Internal dialogue with questions and answers
   - Focused on topic
   - Extensive and intensive

7. Do a PMI (Pluses, Minuses, Interesting Questions) on perceived benefits. Chart the PMI on the board and discuss the "I" responses.

Variations

1. Replace the all-class PMI with a journal entry.
2. Demonstrate a dialogue out loud.

SELF-REVIEW

ACTIVITY-AT-A-GLANCE

Purpose

Review goal-based academic accomplishments using a structured format.

When to Use

Use whenever practice and a format are needed to help students review accomplishments, once a week to review weekly goals, or at the end of a grading period.

What You'll Need

❏ Journals or copies of Self-Review Questions

What to Do

1. Ask students to write one of their academic goals.

2. Introduce or review checking a goal against the "achievable and believable" criteria. (Is it possible to achieve the goal? Does the student have the skills or talents necessary to achieve the goal?)

3. Model the "achievable and believable" criteria with a sample goal.

4. After modeling, invite pairs to share and review their goals using the "achievable and believable" criteria.

5. Provide students with copies of Self-Review Questions or a model to copy in journals, and invite students to write a response to each question.

- *How far have I progressed toward my goal?*
- *What are the barriers I have overcome?*
- *What barriers yet remain?*
- *What help do I need?*

6. After completing all 4 questions, have students meet in pairs to share and review their responses.

7. Following the pair sharing, ask students to select one of the following lead-in statements and write a response in their journals.

- *From this review, I learned . . .*
- *From this review, I am pleased . . .*
- *I intend . . .*

Variations

1. Use a think-pair-share strategy to start this activity.

2. Conclude with a round-robin sharing of responses to lead-in statements.

MY PROBLEM

ACTIVITY-AT-A-GLANCE

Purpose

Become familiar with solving problems through a process and use the Problem-Solving Model as a framework to structure a personal problem-solving process.

When to Use

Use in primary grades to introduce a thematic unit on personal responsibility. With middle school students, use periodically (once a month or more frequently) during an advisor-advisee program or in conjunction with a peer-mediation or conflict-resolution program. Use in secondary classrooms as a tool to help students solve course-related problems.

What You'll Need

❏ Copies of Problem-Solving Model

What to Do

1. Activate students' prior knowledge of problem-solving processes by inviting students to brainstorm a list of approaches or strategies that they use to solve problems. Ask students to identify successful strategies and briefly discuss characteristics successful strategies have in common.

2. Introduce the concept of solving problems through a multistep process. Draw comparisons to student-generated strategies where appropriate.

The Problem	Strategies to Use	The Result
Not getting homework done	1. Write assignments in notebook.	Have a list
	2. Check I have books, etc., at end of day.	Have everything I need
	3. Start homework as soon as I get home.	I'm done before dinner!

3. Show the visual format of the Problem-Solving Model on the board or overhead.

4. Guide the class through the process, asking for a random selection of ideas at each step.

5. Use an all-class round robin to discuss:
   - What was easy to do? Why?
   - What was difficult?
   - Where can this process be used?

6. Distribute copies of the Problem-Solving Model or ask students to copy the format. Ask students to select a hypothetical problem and complete the model.

7. Collect, review, and give feedback on the completed charts. Select 2–3 strong examples to show to the class.

Variations

1. In step 6, have students work in pairs or trios and write group responses on chart paper.

2. In step 7, display student work at different locations in the room and provide students an opportunity to observe and read their classmates' work.

3. Assign a sample topic for all individuals to use.

4. Use the Problem-Solving Model to study content-based problems of individuals or groups in history, social studies, fine arts, etc.

Ideas

IT'S MY CALL

ACTIVITY-AT-A-GLANCE

Purpose

Use a visual organizer as a framework to structure the decision-making process.

When to Use

Use in primary grades to introduce a thematic unit on personal responsibility or decision making. With middle school students, use periodically during an advisor-advisee program or in conjunction with a peer-mediation or conflict-resolution program. Use in secondary classrooms as a tool to help students solve course-related problems.

What You'll Need

❏ No materials necessary

What to Do

1. Activate students' prior knowledge of the decision-making process.

2. Share the purpose of using a visual organizer as a tool to facilitate the decision-making process. Clarify the words: "decisions," "making," and "process."

3. On the overhead or board, show the mind map visual format and invite students to volunteer topics related to decision making. Select a topic (e.g., working in groups) and guide the class through the process of creating a mind map. Be sure to map several choices one can make in deciding how to approach the topic and expected outcomes.

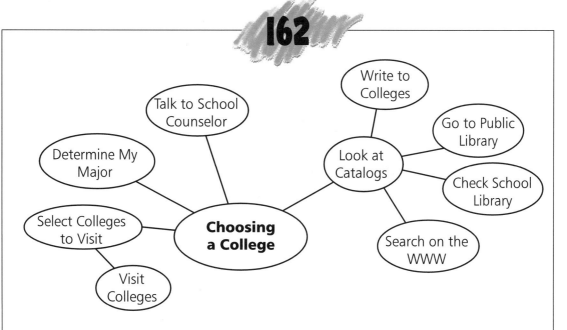

162

Write to Colleges

Talk to School Counselor

Go to Public Library

Determine My Major

Look at Catalogs

Check School Library

Choosing a College

Select Colleges to Visit

Search on the WWW

Visit Colleges

4. Use an all-class round-robin structure to discuss:

   • What was easy to do with this process?

   • What was difficult?

   • What are other topics students could use with this format?

   Use a triple T-chart to list the responses.

Easy	Difficult	Other Topics
Easy to come up with lots of ideas	*Thinking of outcomes*	*Selecting a term paper topic*

5. Invite students to select a topic and use the mind map format to generate ideas and choices related to the topic. Stress the importance of mapping a variety of choices and possible outcomes of each. Monitor and coach as needed.

6. Ask students to write a paragraph summarizing the different options they considered in relation to their topic and to select and describe their most preferred option. Collect, review, and provide feedback.

Variation

Work in pairs or trios to create a mind map on chart paper.

STANDARDS OF EXCELLENCE

ACTIVITY-AT-A-GLANCE

Purpose

Identify individual standards of excellence that can be used to assess academic performance.

When to Use

Use at the beginning of a lesson or unit to introduce the concept of standards or to help students identify their own standards of excellence.

What You'll Need

❑ Coin
❑ Chart paper or posterboards

What to Do

1. Place a coin on the overhead. Ask students to explain or guess how the government knows that this is an acceptable coin. (There is a weight *standard* in the National Bureau of Weights and Standards.)

2. Define the word "standard" based on "flag that rallies troops."

3. Distribute a sheet of chart paper or posterboard to each student.

4. Invite each student to construct a banner that describes his or her own marks of excellence.

5. Allow 30 minutes to complete the banners. Hang banners across the room.

   IRI/SkyLight Training and Publishing, Inc.

6. Each day, encourage at least one student to explain his or her banner to the class.

7. Conclude with a class discussion of:
   - What are "personal" standards?
   - Why are "personal" standards of excellence important?

Variations

1. Replace step 2 with a discussion on identifying characteristics that determine standards. For example, an acceptable coin can be identified by its weight, material, size, and shape.

2. Use trios to identify shared standards.

3. Invite a speaker to share his or her standards of excellence with the class.

4. As a class, compile a list of common shared standards.

5. Hypothesize about personal standards of excellence for historical or literary figures, people in the news, or in terms of requirements for specific careers.

PORTFOLIO

ACTIVITY-AT-A-GLANCE

Purpose

Create a portfolio to use to collect and assess work completed during a course, subject, or over time.

When to Use

Use in classrooms where there is an intent to build student responsibility, or to provide an alternative or supplement to grades as a way of tracking student development.

What You'll Need

- ❏ Construction paper, glue, tape, scissors
- ❏ Sample portfolio
- ❏ Criteria rubric

What to Do

1. Share with the class what a portfolio is (a collection), why it is important (to show progress over a period of time), and how students will use a portfolio (selecting, reflecting on, and assessing the quality of their schoolwork).

2. Show a sample portfolio or a previous student's work. Discuss how the sample artifacts (e.g., tests, essays, individual and group projects, journals, charts, graphs, and other evidences of student's work) were selected and why each was selected (e.g., best, shows improvement, "before" and "after" samples).

3. Share with the class a rubric with the criteria of success that will be used to evaluate the final portfolio (e.g., selection, improvement, organization).

4. Provide the guidelines and a model for construction of the physical portfolio (e.g., size, shape, decorations, material), which students can create either at home or as an in-class assignment. After the first artifact put in the portfolio, provide students the opportunity to do a formal self-assessment using lead-in statements, targeted assessment questions, or a visual organizer. Each time a product is entered, require students to complete and attach an evaluation or self-assessment.

5. At the end of each 6- to 8-week period, instruct students to review the artifacts in the portfolio and select 3–5 entries that meet the established criteria of success. Ask students to write a paragraph describing their selections and why they were chosen. Collect the selected entries and paragraphs, review students' work, and provide written feedback. Invite students to take their portfolios home to share with family members and to invite family members to provide written or oral feedback.

Variations

1. Use portfolios in structured conferences to assess performance and growth over a specified period of time. Use as a springboard for students to establish goals for a new quarter or future work.

2. Use portfolios for group projects.

3. Keep an all-class portfolio. Select the most representative artifact created by individuals or groups from each task, unit, or semester or the best artifact from each student.

4. Use the computer and a CD-ROM to create an electronic portfolio.

LIFE TIMELINE

ACTIVITY-AT-A-GLANCE

Purpose

Use a timeline as a tool to reflect on past, present, and future events of importance in one's life.

When to Use

Use throughout a lesson or unit to help students identify shared celebrations and to help students develop goals based on desired life events (e.g., college graduation). May also use as an icebreaker at the beginning of a school year or quarter.

What You'll Need

❑ Clotheslines and clothespins
❑ Index cards

What to Do

1. Brainstorm with the class a list of significant events in a person's life (e.g., birthdays, high school graduation, etc.).

2. Give each student a clothesline, clothespins, and index cards. Invite students to select 10–15 events that were or that they anticipate will be important in their lives, write each one on an index card, and attach cards to the clothesline in some order.

3. Crisscross the "timelines" across the room.

4. Each day, ask students to mill under the timelines in search of events shared with other persons. Spend 5 minutes to discuss the similarities and differences of past and anticipated events.

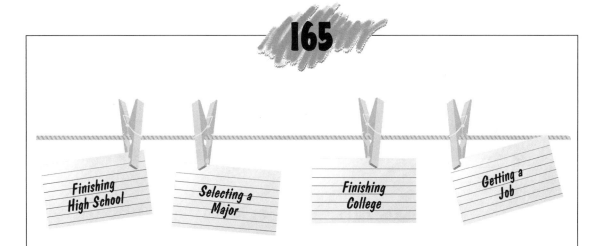

Finishing High School

Selecting a Major

Finishing College

Getting a Job

Variations

1. Stretch yarn or heavy string across a bulletin board or wall in place of hanging clotheslines across the room.

2. Enter individual timelines in a journal.

3. Create timelines on chart paper or 2 pieces of ledger-sized paper taped together. Students can draw in a timeline and paste index cards or attach Post-its to it. Invite students to mill around the room and find 3 persons with similar events and 3 persons with different events and ask these persons to sign their timelines. Conclude activity with a round-robin structure in which students tell something new they learned about one of their classmates.

4. Ask students to prioritize the events of most significance and write a paragraph explaining their choices.

5. Make a homework assignment for students to create a family timeline with their parents and other family members.

6. Use in conjunction with a goal-setting lesson to identify necessary steps to achieve future goals (such as getting a driver's license, passing a test).

PEOPLE INFLUENCES

ACTIVITY-AT-A-GLANCE

Purpose

Reflect on the influences of an important or significant person in one's life.

When to Use

Use as an introduction to a unit or lesson on how significant people affect our lives or as a writing topic in a unit or lesson that teaches paragraph construction and usage.

What You'll Need

❑ Copies of Influence Chart

What to Do

1. Activate prior knowledge of people who have influenced students or are important to them.
2. Form pairs or trios and distribute a copy of the Influence Chart to each group.
3. Explain each column heading. In column 1, students list people important in their lives. In column 2, they tell how the person is related (e.g., brother, aunt, friend). In column 3, students list the reason the person was selected. In column 4, they tell how the person influenced them (e.g., to get good grades, showed me the importance of humor, encouraged me to take a risk). In column 5, students tell what resulted from the influence (e.g., straight-A average, appreciation of humor, joined Pep Club).

Influence Chart

Group Members <u>*Mark, Todd*</u>   Date <u>*Nov. 7*</u>

Important Person	How Related	Why Important	Influence	Result
1. *Aunt Rose*	*Mark's aunt*	*she's special*	*Taught me to appreciate all people.*	*I'm more accepting.*
2. *Frank Lane*	*Todd's teacher*	*believed in me*	*Challenged me to learn more.*	*good grades*
3. *Mike Guzman*	*Mark's coach*	*taught me a lot*	*Showed me the importance of teamwork.*	*I play with the team— not like a solo star.*

4. Invite students to work together as a group to complete the chart. Allow 10–15 minutes for each team to finish its chart. Ask each student to select his or her most significant influence and write a summary paragraph describing this influence.

5. Have students work in groups to share and peer edit the paragraphs.

6. Collect and assess the completed paragraphs.

Variations

1. Do as an individual activity.

2. Instead of a paragraph, ask each group to draw 2–3 valid conclusions from its chart and present these to the whole class.

3. For middle school and secondary students, assign a 3–5 paragraph essay describing the people who are or have been the major influences in their lives.

CAREER LADDER

ACTIVITY-AT-A-GLANCE

Purpose

Explore and prioritize career decisions.

When to Use

Use to encourage students to explore career options and to encourage students to think in terms of priorities.

What You'll Need

❏ Journals

What to Do

1. Draw a ladder on an overhead or board. Ask students to identify possible uses of a ladder. Explain using a ladder graphic as a visual tool to identify and set priorities.

2. Brainstorm a list of careers with the students.

3. Ask a volunteer to select 3 careers and enter his or her choices on the ladder graphic. Ask the student to explain or defend his or her priorities.

4. Have each student repeat these steps in his or her journal.

5. After the ranking step is done, invite each student to write a letter to his or her parent(s) explaining the choices.

6. Have pairs edit and proofread the letters before the students take them home.

Dear Mom,

Someday I would love to be a famous potter. I know, though, that it will take many years to become skilled at this craft and I don't want to starve in the meantime. I've been con- sidering possible careers and have decided that I want to become a graphic artist.

Variations

1. Substitute "goals for continuous improvement," "goals for this school year," or "goals for lifelong learning" in place of possible careers.

2. Review, select, and post a variety of examples.

SEASONAL LETTER

ACTIVITY-AT-A-GLANCE

Purpose

Write a letter to a grandparent, relative, or older person about an interesting personal experience related to a particular season of the year.

When to Use

Use throughout a lesson or unit to encourage students to write from personal experience or as the culmination of a unit on letter writing. Also can use to promote dialogue and sharing across generations and with family members.

What You'll Need

❏ A copy of "Thanksgiving Day" by Lydia Maria Child (First line is "Over the river and through the wood.")

What to Do

1. Play the song or read the words to "Thanksgiving Day."

2. Ask students how many have gone to visit a grandparent. What was the experience like? What do they remember about their grandparents?

3. Review the task. Students are to write a letter to a grandparent (who may or may not be living) or an older relative or adult in their neighborhood. In the letter, students are to describe an interesting personal experience that happened in a particular season of the year.

Dear Grandpa,
I'm looking forward to visiting
you over spring break. I hope
there isn't a surprise blizzard
like there was two years ago.
Did I ever tell you about that?
I was at the airport with Dad
and Zach.

4. As a class, brainstorm ideas. Share a personal example or solicit student examples.

5. Ask students to select an experience and then form pairs for a prewriting activity. In pairs, students take turns describing who they will be writing to, the experience and seasonal connection, and why it was chosen.

6. Students work individually to write letters. Upon completion, use pairs to proofread letters, check proper form, punctuation, spelling, etc.

7. If the grandparent, relative, or older person is living, send a copy of the letter.

Variations

1. After the topic brainstorm, list age-appropriate criteria for a well-written letter.

2. Invite students to read the poem to their parents and ask them to tell a personal experience about a family trip to a relative or a seasonal-related experience they had when they were children. Provide an opportunity for students to share their family stories in small groups or with the whole class.

GOAL CHART

ACTIVITY-AT-A-GLANCE

Purpose

Set goals and align tasks using a chart format.

When to Use

Use when students need to establish a regular, systematic goal process at regular times each day or week or when students need to have a structure for thinking through and assessing their goals.

What You'll Need

❑ Copies of Goal Chart

What to Do

1. Do a prior knowledge check about goals. After the check, highlight the concept that goals are targets or aims that one wants to achieve. Personal goals can relate to family, friends, schoolwork, sports, interests, etc.

2. On the board or overhead, display the Goal Chart.

3. Demonstrate the process of selecting and ranking goals by filling in the chart with examples.

4. Group students in pairs and give each student a copy of the Goal Chart. Instruct students to spend 3–5 minutes talking about their goals or listening to their partner, and then to reverse roles.

Goal Chart

	Goal	Rank	Why Important	How to Achieve	Checkup	By When
1.	Pass keyboarding	3	I need to know how to use a computer	Practice more	every Friday	end of semester
2.	Participate in all track meets	2	Running makes me feel great	Rearrange job schedule; get all homework done early	every Friday	ongoing until June
3.	Save $300 for a car	4	Would make getting around easier	Save 50% of every paycheck	in a month	by June 1
4.	Make Dean's List	1	Want to do my best, plus it'll help me get in a good college	Study, work hard, do all assignments	every Friday	end of semester
5.	Select 2–3 colleges to visit	5	Need to learn more about colleges	Review catalogs, talk to guidance counselor	in a month	by June 1

5. After both partners have discussed their goals, they list identified goals in column 1 and, working together, complete the rest of their individual charts. Remind pairs to share in confidence and to keep confidentiality.

6. At the end of each week (or designated time period), use pairs to review progress, adjust or add goals, and adjust "how" and timelines.

Variations

1. Eliminate pairs and make this an individual reflective task.

2. Invite students to share goals and plans with the class.

3. Limit the chart's focus (e.g., academic goals for this course).

PLUS OR MINUS

ACTIVITY-AT-A-GLANCE

Purpose

Use a visual organizer as a tool to assess progress and achievements.

When to Use

Use after students have learned to set goals to structure goal or task assessment, when doing a task such as a project, essay, or lab report, or throughout a lesson or unit to track progress.

What You'll Need

❑ Journals

What to Do

1. On the board or overhead, display the Plus or Minus T-chart.
2. Model completing the chart with a goal or task related to teaching responsibilities (e.g., preparing a bulletin board). What were the pluses and minuses of how this task was done?
3. Ask students to copy the Plus or Minus T-chart in their journals or on paper. Invite students to select a goal or task they are working on and to complete the chart. Review goal criteria.
4. Collect completed charts and provide feedback.

Plus or Minus

Goal or Task   *Having students create bulletin board display*

Pluses	Minuses
1. *Stimulates students' interest in topic.*	1. *Have to do after class.*
2. *Engages students as partners in learning.*	2. *May not be as comprehensive as desired.*
3. *Provides fresh perspective.*	3. *Requires supervision.*

Variations

1. Use the chart to assess the pluses and minuses of the goal or task itself.
2. Share charts in pairs.
3. Use the chart with team goals.

AUTOBIOGRAPHY

ACTIVITY-AT-A-GLANCE

Purpose

Examine characteristics of an autobiography and write an autobiography.

When to Use

Use throughout a lesson or unit to expand students' writing abilities.

What You'll Need

❏ Sample autobiography
❏ Post-it notes or index cards

What to Do

1. Begin with a study of an appropriate autobiography.

2. Using the studied example, identify the characteristics of a successful autobiography. For instance:

   • Personal story

   • Incidents reveal character

   • Interesting pace

   • Connected incidents

   • Influence of background

3. Use a sequence chart or timeline to model an arrangement of important life events. Use examples from studied autobiography or own life history.

4. Invite students to write and sequence their life histories. Ask students to write individual events on Post-it notes or index cards. Demonstrate to students how to expand the events. (Primary students may write 1 or 2 descriptive sentences for each event. Middle school students may write a paragraph. Secondary students may write several paragraphs or pages on each event.)

5. Explain sequencing events by using a chart or timeline format.

6. Expand the sequence chart or timeline to include a sketch or drawing for each selected event.

7. Bend or staple the completed work and have each student title his or her autobiography.

8. Assess each student's finished work according to the selected criteria.

Variations

1. Introduce a peer-editing step before the final draft.

2. Focus on a specific aspect of a student's life such as an academic autobiography or talent autobiography.

DECISION LETTER

ACTIVITY-AT-A-GLANCE

Purpose

Practice letter-writing skills using an incident revolving around an important decision.

When to Use

Use during a lesson or unit to encourage students to establish their own criteria for success.

What You'll Need

❑ Sample letter

What to Do

1. Show a model letter on the overhead or give each student a copy of a selected letter. Review the formal parts and structure of a letter (i.e., address, date, salutation, etc.) and the criteria for success (e.g., grammar, structure, punctuation, spelling, interest, clarity). Ask students to evaluate the sample letter based on the established criteria.

2. Assign students to write a two-page letter to a friend about an important decision they've made. Review how this is done.

3. As a class or in small groups, brainstorm a list of ideas for the students' decisions and topics. Following this activity, students write their first drafts.

4. In pairs, students peer edit first drafts. They then write a second draft. Monitor and coach students as necessary. If possible, arrange to meet with students for a short conference either upon completion of the first draft or at any time during the writing process.

5. Collect final copies and review. Select examples that match the criteria and read several to the class.

Variations

1. Change the letter's topic to decisions made by historic or literary figures, school or community issues, or positions held on current events issues.

2. Pair students and invite students to write a letter to their partner. Exchange letters and write a letter in response. Post sets of letters or meet in small groups to share them.

SCHOOL SUPPORT LETTER

ACTIVITY-AT-A-GLANCE

Purpose

Reflect on the benefits of school and assess individual progress.

When to Use

Use throughout the school year to help improve students' assessment skills.

What You'll Need

- ❏ Model persuasive essay
- ❏ Copies of an assessment tool such as the PMI or Mrs. Potter's Questions

What to Do

1. Ask students to use a PMI or other assessment tool to evaluate the benefits of attending their school or participating in a particular school program.

2. Assign students to write an essay that argues a supportive position for the school or a special program in which they participate. The essay *must communicate the benefits from personal experience.*

3. Establish expectations for the completed essay. Show students a model persuasive essay and ask them to identify examples that illustrate the established criteria for success on this task.

4. Use base groups or pairs to develop ideas for the topics. After 10 minutes, use a group round-robin structure to create a list of ideas.

5. In class, coach students in the selection and development of their essays. Assign first draft for homework.

6. Use base groups or pairs to peer edit the first draft and develop a PMI assessment of each essay.

7. Collect and review the drafts and assessments. Provide individual or all-class feedback prior to students writing final drafts.

8. Require students to attach an individual PMI or other self-assessment to their final copies.

Variations

1. Use to assist students in the creation of a persuasive essay. Vary the length from 1 paragraph to a full-blown, multiparagraph essay appropriate to the students' ages and writing expertise.

2. Change the topic to one in which students have very strong feelings (e.g., school uniforms, abolishing or expanding amount of homework, lengthening the school year). Assign students to write an essay on the benefits or drawbacks of a particular position by drawing on their own personal experiences. Upon completion, students pair with a classmate with the opposite perspective and share letters.

3. Use Variation 2 to prepare for a class debate.

INTERNET HOBBY SEARCH

ACTIVITY-AT-A-GLANCE

Purpose

Use the Internet to deepen personal interest and knowledge of a hobby.

When to Use

Use throughout a lesson or unit to encourage students to expand their range of interests and talents.

What You'll Need

❏ Computers
❏ Internet access
❏ Copies of Internet Hobby Search

What to Do

1. Create a web with the word "hobby." Ask students to describe what a hobby is. Select the most critical attributes.

2. Pair students to discuss what hobbies each has and what they like about their hobbies. After a 3–5 minute discussion, call for volunteers to contribute to a class list of hobbies.

3. Provide each student with a copy of Internet Hobby Search. Review rules for Internet use.

4. Collect copies and review students' work. Provide feedback and assist students in preparing presentations.

Internet Hobby Search

1. What are your special interests?
   art, crafts, design

2. What are your special talents?
   freeform drawing, eye for color

3. What hobbies do you have that match your interests or talents?
   batiking, sewing, tie-dyeing

4. What hobbies would you like to learn more about?
   batiking

5. Pick one hobby and using the Internet identify resources for learning about this hobby.
   1. Custom Colors Company   2. Creative Clothes   3. Batik-It

Select 2–5 resources. Study them and prepare a 3–5 minute talk that describes the hobby, explains talents and/or skills needed for this hobby, and tells what your personal interest in this hobby is and how it might benefit you.

5. Conduct student talks or presentations. Before the talks start, provide evaluation criteria.

Variations

1. If students don't have Internet access, use the school or local library for resource identification and to access resource materials.

2. After students have completed their research, have students form groups of 3–5. Ask students to discuss what they have learned about their hobbies and brainstorm a list of questions that would apply to all of the group's hobbies (e.g., What materials are used?). Using these questions and each student's hobby, have students create a group matrix.

3. In place of a class talk, give students the option either to write a multiparagraph essay or share information verbally in pairs or trios.

MRS. POTTER'S QUESTIONS

 ACTIVITY-AT-A-GLANCE

Purpose

Use a critiquing process to assess academic performance and/or the effects of personal decisions.

When to Use

After the process is demonstrated, practiced, and checked, use the questions as a conclusion to any assignment, lesson, or unit to focus on the *process* of the task to encourage self-assessment; on a scheduled basis each week or month in conjunction with a journal and course-specific skills; or to assess the portfolio-selection process on a quarterly basis.

What You'll Need

❏ List of Mrs. Potter's Questions

What to Do

1. On the board, overhead, or a bulletin board, display Mrs. Potter's Questions. (Editor's note: Mrs. Potter is a teacher who uses these questions to help her students assess their performance. For additional information on Mrs. Potter's Questions, see *Patterns for Thinking, Patterns for Transfer,* Bellanca and Fogarty, 1993.)

2. Introduce questions as a tool students can use on a regular basis to assess their performance. Describe the different ways this can be done (e.g., journal, post-task writing activity, pair discussion).

> ## Mrs. Potter's Questions
>
> - **What was I expected to do?**
> - **What did I do well?**
> - **If I did the same task again, what would I do differently?**
> - **What help do I need?**

3. Using an example from personal experience (e.g., how I prepare for class or how I grade student portfolios), demonstrate answering each question.

4. Use the example to highlight "indicators of excellence," or overall standards that you have have previously identified and communicated to students. For example:

   - Uses at least 3 specific examples for each question.
   - Shows insight into personal strengths and sees areas to improve.
   - Spells correctly.
   - Uses complete and/or grammatically correct sentences.

5. Provide an age-appropriate topic for a whole-class demonstration. For example:

   - Primary—doing my homework.
   - Middle—cleaning my room.
   - Secondary—saying no to alcohol or drug pressures.

6. Set discussion guidelines to ensure receptive climate.

7. Invite student responses to each question. Record the responses on the board or overhead.

8. Review the process with a four-column T-chart on board or overhead. Encourage multiple responses.

Expected to Do	Did Well	Do Differently	Help
Clean my room	Put stuff away in closet and drawers	Clean out closet and drawers first	How to organize things better— ask my mom

9. Use the "Help" column to list specific concerns. Encourage students to respond to each item in the "Help" column before adding additional items (e.g., How can you get the help you need? Who can you ask for help?).

10. Check for understanding. Assign a home or in-class assignment that will conclude with students responding to Mrs. Potter's Questions.

Variations

1. Use as a process introduction. Instead of teaching all 4 steps together, do 1 step at a time until all students grasp the concept.

2. Invite students to use prior to midterm (or other checkpoint) student-teacher conferences to assess progress and performance.

NATURALIST

GARDENING PROJECT

ACTIVITY-AT-A-GLANCE

Purpose
Create and care for a garden.

When to Use
In primary grades, use as a botany unit integrated with mathematics and language arts. In middle grades, use as an investigative unit of the growing cycle.

What You'll Need
❑ Open land or garden plots
❑ Seeds or seedlings (several different types)
❑ Gardening tools, string, fertilizer, yardsticks or tape measures

What to Do

1. Use a prior knowledge identifier (such as the KWL) to determine what students know about gardens.

2. Introduce the project, creating a class garden, and brainstorm what students might learn from the experience (e.g., mathematics, geometry, counting, measurement, etc.).

3. Form groups of 3 students each. Preview the tasks each group will do: measuring the plot; laying out the plot for 4 items (by rows or quarters); tilling the plot; and preparing the soil (using proper fertilizer for soil type). Identify the land to be used (ideally, a

IRI/SkyLight Training and Publishing, Inc.

5' x 5' plot for each group). The space needs easy access, good protection, and relative ease of use.

4. Provide planning time for students to select what they will plant and how. Have students identify appropriate roles or tasks (e.g., recorder, leader, tools manager) and select roles/tasks for each group member.

5. Provide students a selection of seeds or transplants (4 types per group) with planting and watering instructions. Start gardening by preparing the soil and designing the plots.

6. Encourage students to keep a gardening journal in which they record information about their gardening activities (e.g., types of soil, effects of mixing, annual life of the soil, weather conditions, effects of fertilizing). Provide students opportunities to share and discuss their observations, both in small groups and as a class.

7. Make weekly (or more frequent) visits to the plots for thinning plants, tending the soil, weeding, watering, and fertilizing. Students should continue recording observations of the growing cycle and factors affecting growth (e.g., weather, fertilizer). Hold weekly discussions about their observations.

8. Harvest the crops and send samples home.

9. Revisit the goals of the project and make a class list of what was learned.

Variations

1. Record weather conditions and observed stages of growth in a comparison or relational chart.

2. Draw observed stages of growth for each plant and chart growth rates.

OBSERVATION SKETCHES

ACTIVITY-AT-A-GLANCE

Purpose

Enhance observation skills of natural objects.

When to Use

Use when introducing students to scientific observations, at the beginning of lab units when starting botany or zoology projects, or as closure to a biology unit.

What You'll Need

❏ Sketch paper, colored pencils, erasers
❏ Dried flowers, leaves, or plants

What to Do

1. Ensure that each student has a box of colored pencils, eraser, sketch paper, and a single dried flower, leaf, or plant.

2. Using the overhead or board, demonstrate how to observe a sample flower. Have students look at the flower's colors, shape, lines, angles, size, patterns, etc., and list their observations. Demonstrate the replication process by drawing the sample as accurately as possible.

3. Invite students to study their specimens and list the features they observe. Ask them to sketch their flower, leaf, or plant as completely and accurately as possible.

4. Display completed sketches.

IRI/SkyLight Training and Publishing, Inc.

5. As a class, discuss what was challenging and what was easy to do in this activity. Use a T-chart to record responses.

6. Conclude activity by asking students to write a paragraph using a lead-in statement such as *When I observe, I . . .* or *When I draw what I observe, I . . .*

Variations

1. Use a single plant, flower, or leaf for all to observe and sketch.

2. Use pairs for the observation step. Each pair will make a single list.

3. Ask students to draw an object using a list of observations created by another person. Once the drawing is complete, compare it to the actual object. Pair students so that the "observer" and "sketcher" can review the list of observations and drawing and identify the accuracy of sketched features and what additional information would have helped the sketcher to draw a more accurate representation of the object.

CLASSIFICATION MATRIX

ACTIVITY-AT-A-GLANCE

Purpose

Classify items using a visual organizer.

When to Use

Use during a lesson or unit to teach students how to distinguish characteristics of items, to teach students the meaning of classification, and to enable students to make generalizations about items based on shared attributes.

What You'll Need

❑ Copies of a matrix

What to Do

1. Display a matrix on the board or overhead. Select a family or group of items related to a specific unit being studied (e.g., trees, planets). Label each column with a characteristic or category that can be used to describe (or classify) the items. List individual items in the far left column.

2. Explain the meaning of "classification" and demonstrate how to enter identifying features for each item onto the matrix.

3. Ask students to complete individual matrixes as they study the topic. Provide opportunities throughout the unit to add items to the matrixes.

Animals

	How They Move	Where They Live	Type of Blood	A Unique Characteristic
Birds	Fly	Land	Warm Blooded	Wings
Fish	Swim	Water	Warm or Cold Blooded	Gills
Mammals	Walk	Land or Water	Warm Blooded	Drink Mother's Milk

4. As a class, discuss what "thinking" steps students used as they completed the matrixes.

Variations

1. Use cooperative groups to complete the matrixes.

2. Provide small groups of students several related items (e.g., leaves, books, buttons). Ask students to identify characteristics that can be used to categorize the items (e.g., shape, type of book, number of button holes) and to label the matrix columns accordingly. Next, list each item in the far left column and, working as a group, complete the matrix.

3. Follow up with more complex items that require higher-level classification skills.

PLANT OBSERVATIONS

ACTIVITY-AT-A-GLANCE

Purpose

Deepen or develop observation skills in conjunction with growing plants.

When to Use

Use during a lesson or unit to introduce students to the importance of observation in the science field, to help older students learn care and precision in making observations, and to introduce the growth cycle of plants.

What You'll Need

- ❏ Posterboards or chart paper
- ❏ Variety of seeds, pots, potting soil

What to Do

1. Provide each student with seeds from 3 different plants: a flower, a weed, and a legume. Give each student 3 soil pots and potting soil.

2. Ask students to make charts that they will use to show the growth cycle of each plant. To start, students sketch each seed, using actual size and dimension, and label each drawing. Students can chart each plant either horizontally or vertically, but need to allow space for numerous other entries (both sketches and written descriptions) to be made during the growth cycle of the plants.

3. Discuss what must happen for the seeds to grow (e.g., plant them, water them, provide sunlight). Ask students to create a list of growing instructions for each plant.

4. Ask students to examine their plants on alternate days for signs of growth and to record their observations on their charts. Students may record their observations by sketching what they see or through short written descriptions.

5. After the plants are 6–7 weeks old, have students create an all-class chart or matrix listing common features they observe for each plant. Follow up with additional matrixes and/or charts at different stages of the growing cycle. In addition, create charts that show how each plant is similar to the others and how it is different. Emphasize accuracy and completeness of observations.

6. Once plants have reached a fairly mature stage, ask students to write summaries that describe the characteristics of each plant at various stages of the growing cycle.

Variations

1. Use pairs or trios for this task. Designate roles such as observer, recorder, and encourager. For each chart activity, students alternate roles so that each student has a chance to observe, record, and encourage. (Role variations also can include drawer and writer.)

2. Upon completion of all charts, students select 1 plant and create posters that describe the growth cycle of that plant. Students can incorporate existing drawings, charts, and written notations or create new ones.

3. Create a class portfolio or book for each plant that includes student sketches, charts, and written descriptions of each plant at various stages of the growing cycle.

WHAT IS THE PROBLEM?

ACTIVITY-AT-A-GLANCE

Purpose

Sharpen ability to identify a scientific problem.

When to Use

Use in a lesson or unit to introduce students to problem-solving methods.

What You'll Need

❏ Copies of letters or memos that represent different points of view on a specific topic

What to Do

1. Form groups of 5 students each. Give each group a letter or memo about a current community issue (e.g., chemicals in the drinking water, leaf burning). Each letter should represent a unique point of view. Ask students to imagine that they are a committee that will advise a local commissioner on how to resolve the problem. However, before they can recommend any solutions, they need to agree on the nature of the problem.

2. Ask groups to read their letters, discuss the issue, and form a consensus on what the problem is and how best to solve it. Request that groups present this information to the class and explain their reasoning.

3. After all presentations are complete, mediate a discussion regarding which methods and reasons were appropriate for identifying the problem and recommending solutions.

4. List problem-identification criteria on the board or overhead.

Variations

1. Provide copies of all letters to each group.

2. Do in conjunction with a lesson on persuasive writing.

3. Provide the class with a set of "problem" criteria to contrast with their ideas.

SCIENCE INTERVIEW

ACTIVITY-AT-A-GLANCE

Purpose

Develop interviewing skills as a means of gathering and organizing information.

When to Use

Use in conjunction with a research project that requires students to obtain firsthand, or direct, information, during a lesson or unit on research skills, or as an introduction for an essay assignment.

What You'll Need

❏ Copies of background information on different scientists or inventors

What to Do

1. Ask students to brainstorm a list of questions a television talk show host could use to interview guests. Display on board or overhead.

2. Explain the activity. Each student will interview another student to obtain information on a scientist or inventor and use this information to write an essay. Each student also will be interviewed about a different scientist or inventor and provide information for the interviewer to write a report.

3. Assign each student 2 scientists or inventors. One will be the subject that the student needs to obtain information about; the other will be the subject that the student will be interviewed about. Provide background information on the latter person.

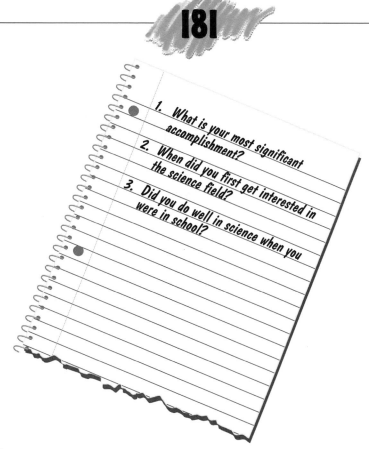

181

1. What is your most significant accomplishment?
2. When did you first get interested in the science field?
3. Did you do well in science when you were in school?

4. Ask students to construct a list of questions to use during the interviews.

5. Pair up students and have one student interview the other to obtain information on his or her assigned subject, then reverse roles. Ask students to write individual essays using the information they obtained from their interviews.

6. Follow up with a discussion that examines the interviewing process and the value of using questions in an interview for collecting accurate information.

Variations

1. Use historic or literary figures as the subjects for the essays.

2. Assign a position paper on a topic related to community or global concerns or environmental issues. Ask students to interview one of their family members or a friend to obtain information and to use this information to write their essays.

AHA! LOG

ACTIVITY-AT-A-GLANCE

Purpose

Learn how to make process notes during a scientific inquiry.

When to Use

Use during a long-term science lab experiment or one that will occur over several class periods.

What You'll Need

❑ Videotape on Leonardo da Vinci or Charles Darwin, VCR
❑ Notebooks

What to Do

1. Introduce students to the notebooks of Leonardo da Vinci or Charles Darwin. (Videotapes about their scientific accomplishments most likely will show how they kept their logs.)

2. Ask students to use a notebook to log information during a lab experiment. Instruct students to include the following for each log entry: date, topic of study, sketch or written description of the day's lab topic, notes on procedures used, and at least one "aha!" gained from the experiment. ("Aha," or eureka, refers to an exclamation made when a person discovers something or when a confusing concept or fact suddenly becomes clear.)

3. Select 5–6 logs daily to collect and read. Provide brief commentary or feedback.

4. At the end of the experiment, instruct students to review their logs and make a closing entry about the log process and their own reactions to it. (For example, Describe the most important thing you learned during this process. Has keeping a log been an advantage or disadvantage to you? Why?)

Variations

1. Provide opportunities for informal or small group sharing of logs throughout the process.

2. Select student sketches and transfer them to overhead transparencies. As a class, discuss strengths of displayed sketches.

3. Use logs during literature or music classes to record daily "ahas."

4. Introduce by explaining the concept of "ahas," or eurekas, and ask students to reflect on prior experiences and recall a significant eureka. Invite students to share their experiences.

SCIENCE VENN

ACTIVITY-AT-A-GLANCE

Purpose

Compare and contrast natural phenomena using a Venn diagram.

When to Use

Use to compare and contrast similar phenomena in a science unit.

What You'll Need

❏ Objects for comparison

What to Do

1. Ask 2 students to stand in the front of the room. Draw a Venn diagram with 2 interlinked circles and label the circles with the students' names. Ask the class to identify ways in which the students are similar and ways in which they are different. Ask a recorder to list differences in the appropriate circle and to list similarities in the area shared by, or the intersection of, both circles.

2. Display 2 versions of the same object (e.g., microscopes, globes, triangles) and ask students to create Venn diagrams that show their shared and unique characteristics.

3. When students have finished their diagrams, create an all-class Venn diagram that incorporates all the characteristics noted by the class.

4. Select material from the textbook that allows for visual and verbal comparison (e.g., African vs. Asian elephants, deciduous trees vs. conifer trees). Instruct students to construct a Venn diagram from this text material. Review the results.

IRI/SkyLight Training and Publishing, Inc.

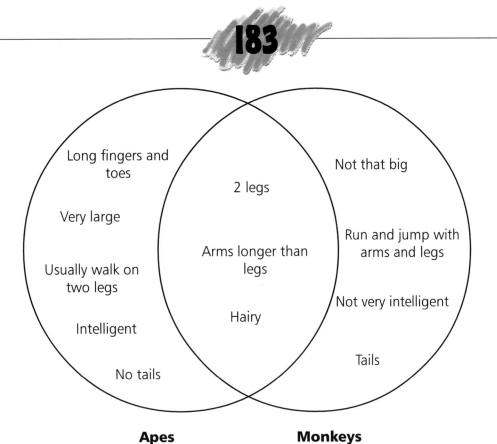

Long fingers and toes

Very large

Usually walk on two legs

Intelligent

No tails

2 legs

Arms longer than legs

Hairy

Not that big

Run and jump with arms and legs

Not very intelligent

Tails

Apes   **Monkeys**

5. Close with a discussion that identifies the criteria for a successful Venn diagram, when it is useful to use Venn diagrams, and the value of Venn diagrams in naturalist study.

Variations

1. Use pairs or trios to construct the Venn diagrams.

2. Increase the number of objects compared.

3. Use Venn diagrams in other content areas (e.g., comparing literary characters or historic periods).

SCIENCE NEWS

ACTIVITY-AT-A-GLANCE

Purpose

Write summaries of naturalistic observations.

When to Use

Use during an interdisciplinary unit involving science and writing, to connect students' observations of nature with appropriate conclusions, or to develop or enhance students' observation skills.

What You'll Need

❏ Access to land with diverse plant life
❏ Clipboards, paper, pencils or pens, pegs or sticks
❏ Sample essay

What to Do

1. Assign students an "in-the-field" observation task: to examine a specific plot of land, identify at least 3 samples of a plant species growing in it, and report their findings through written descriptions and sketches.

2. Go to an outdoor area that has a variety of plants. Mark off the boundaries of specific plots by having students walk around the areas they will study. Use sticks or pegs to show boundaries.

3. Provide each student with a clipboard, paper, and pens or pencils. Review the terms (e.g., flora, species, etc.) appropriate to the assignment. Ask students to find 3 samples of the group, sketch the identifying features of each item, and label each sketch.

4. Upon return to the classroom, present a model 3–5 paragraph essay. Review its parts: introduction and detail paragraphs describing the key features observed and the locale of the observation. Ask students to write descriptions of their findings as if they were addressing scientific readers in search of a new discovery. Use small groups or a peer-editing process to review first drafts, edit, and revise.

5. Upon completion, form groups of 6–8 students each. Distribute essays and ask each group to select reports from other students and create a newspaper with name, headlines, etc. Post the completed editions.

Variations

1. Group students into observation teams for outside study.

2. Vary the type of site (e.g., prairie, forest, backyard garden).

3. Conduct observations of the same site at different times of the year. Create new editions of the newspaper to report on seasonal differences.

PREDICTION CHECK

ACTIVITY-AT-A-GLANCE

Purpose
Develop and practice prediction skills in relation to scientific topics.

When to Use
Use when introducing the use of prediction in science experiments.

What You'll Need
❏ Coin
❏ Individual-sized cereal boxes (5 per group)
❏ Sets of similar items with unknown quantities of contents

What to Do

1. Invite a student to take a coin and stand in front of the class. Have other students, one at a time, "call" a coin flip. Assign a student to record each "heads" or "tails" call and post the result on the board or overhead.

2. After 25–30 tosses, ask several students to predict the next 5 tosses and explain the rationale for their choices. Test their predictions.

3. Ask students to identify what it takes to make a "probable" prediction, that is, one likely to happen (sufficient, accurate data in a repeated pattern). Identify when predictions are used (e.g., waiting for a bus, weather forecasts). Describe probability guidelines.

4. Form groups of 3 students each. Give each group 5 individual-sized boxes of cereal. (Each person in a group must have the same type of cereal. Different groups may have different types of cereals.) Instruct groups to predict the number of cereal pieces in each box. After the first box, test their predictions by counting out the pieces. Repeat for the remaining boxes using established probability guidelines.

5. Review each group's predictions. Discuss and determine which were valid. Review the probability guidelines and repeat the task with another set of items.

Variation

Use musical notation from a popular song to show predictable patterning.

INTERNSHIP

ACTIVITY-AT-A-GLANCE

Purpose

Gain direct experience working in a science-related profession.

When to Use

Use after the first semester or quarter with secondary students who have taken science classes or have science-related work experience.

What You'll Need

❏ List of available internships in community
❏ Journals

What to Do

1. Provide interested students with a list of open internships within the local science community (e.g., botanical gardens, missions, university science departments, the school's science department, local manufacturing companies with in-house labs).

2. Arrange interviews for the students. Ask students to prepare for interviews by writing questions to ask to identify their roles, responsibilities, job expectations, and criteria for success during the internships. Have students role play the interviewing process.

3. Ask students who obtain internships to keep journals of their experiences. Provide targeted questions or topics for different checkpoints of their internships (e.g., first impressions, description of work done in the company or department, the most important thing learned). During the internship, visit the site, observe the student, and confer with the student and supervisor.

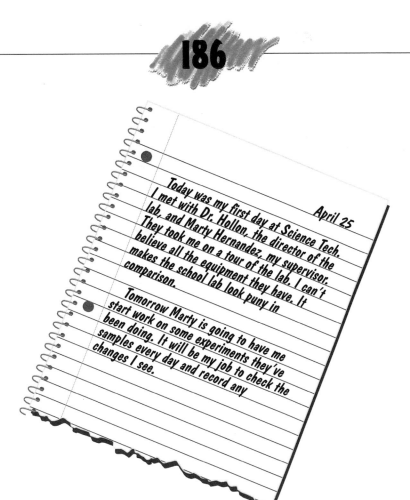

186

Today was my first day at Science Tech. I met with Dr. Hollon, the director of the lab, and Marty Hernandez, my supervisor. They took me on a tour of the lab. I can't believe all the equipment they have. It makes the school lab look puny in comparison.

April 25

Tomorrow Marty is going to have me start work on some experiments they've been doing. It will be my job to check the samples every day and record any changes I see.

Variations

1. Let interested students seek their own internship sites.

2. Assign students to research (through interviews) a person working in a science-related profession. Brainstorm a master list of interview questions related to the type of work the person does, requirements of the job (such as education, skills, and aptitude), working conditions, and satisfactions or drawbacks of the job. Allow students to present their information as a written report, in a journal or newsletter format, or on videotape.

NATURE DIRECTIONS

ACTIVITY-AT-A-GLANCE

Purpose

Use physical landmarks and geographical features to provide directions to a specific location.

When to Use

Use at the beginning of the school year or course to focus attention on the natural environment and to sharpen students' observation skills.

What You'll Need

❏ Sketch paper

What to Do

1. Ask for 2–3 volunteers to describe the route they take from their homes to the school. After their responses, ask if they could describe the route without using any street names and using only geographical features (e.g., hill, trees, rock). Ask a volunteer to draw a map using only geographical features on the board or overhead. As a class, brainstorm a list of geographical features and physical landmarks (e.g., buildings, fences) that can be used to provide directions.

2. Ask students to draw maps that illustrate the route from their homes to the school. Instruct them to use pictures or symbols only (no words allowed) to represent geographical features and landmarks. Stress the need for specificity and clarity.

3. Share maps and display. Follow up with a group discussion to review the activity and students' reactions. Ask students when this type of map would be especially helpful.

Variations

1. Ask students to draw maps from one specific point in the schoolyard (or other outdoor area) to another using only geographical features and physical markers. Randomly distribute completed maps and have students use the provided directions to move from one location to another.

2. Use in conjunction with a literature selection that provides detailed setting descriptions. Ask students to draw maps that show a particular area or locality.

3. Combine with a study on topographical features of maps.

CAUSE AND EFFECT

ACTIVITY-AT-A-GLANCE

Purpose

Analyze cause-and-effect relationships by using a graphic organizer.

When to Use

Use during a lesson or unit with curriculum material that calls for or demonstrates the importance of cause-and-effect analysis or when a situation arises in a lab experiment that calls for a cause-effect analysis.

What You'll Need

❑ Model of fishbone diagram

What to Do

1. Identify prior knowledge of cause-and-effect relationships.

2. Display the fishbone diagram on the board or overhead. Demonstrate how to use the diagram to illustrate cause and effect. For example, select an environmental-related problem or effect, such as polluted beaches, and write this in the "effect" box (fish's head). List primary causes on the diagonal bones of the fish's skeleton. Record supporting evidence or facts on the secondary (or horizontal) bones. Review the entire diagram to understand how the elements that comprise the fish's skeleton contribute to or cause the effect.

3. Ask students to select a content-related topic (e.g., energy flow cut off, photosynthesis) and create a fishbone diagram to show the cause-and-effect relationship. Share completed diagrams as a class.

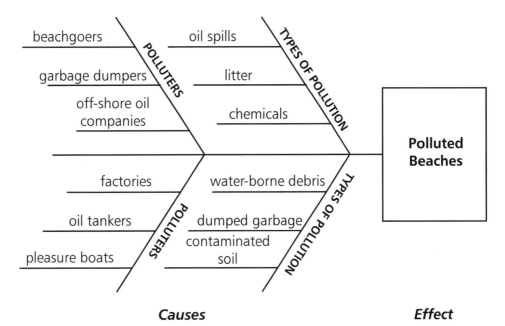

beachgoers

POLLUTERS

oil spills

TYPES OF POLLUTION

garbage dumpers

litter

off-shore oil
companies

chemicals

**Polluted
Beaches**

factories

water-borne debris

TYPES OF POLLUTION

oil tankers

dumped garbage

POLLUTERS

pleasure boats

contaminated
soil

Causes

Effect

4. Close with a discussion of what students learned about cause-
and-effect relationships and when they might use this tool.

Variations

1. Use cooperative groups to complete the fishbone diagrams.
2. Use in conjunction with a history or literature lesson. Have students
   identify a problem, effect, or outcome (e.g., Civil War) and list causes
   and contributing factors on the fishbones.

189

SCIENCE EXHIBITION

ACTIVITY-AT-A-GLANCE

Purpose

Create a science exhibit at the end of a unit or semester of scientific study.

When to Use

Use at the end of a major lesson, unit, or semester to provide students opportunities to use their cumulative knowledge to display information in a public forum.

What You'll Need

- ❏ Videotape on a world's fair or exhibition, VCR
- ❏ Books and information on science fairs
- ❏ Sample exhibit(s)

What to Do

1. Activate students' prior knowledge about exhibitions (such as at museums, the Epcot Center, science fairs). Discuss the purpose of an exhibition. Show students a videotape about the world's fair or other exhibitions.

2. Assign the creation of a science exhibit well in advance of its due date. Provide criteria for success (e.g., a single idea, data chart, visual display, etc.). Show samples of exhibits from previous classes and highlight the notable qualities.

3. As a class, brainstorm a list of topics or ideas that could be used for the science exhibit (e.g., Tinkertoys that show energy flow, a chemical reaction). Post the list in a visible spot for reference by students needing ideas. Provide books on science exhibitions for reference as well.

4. Define expectations for time devoted to the exhibits and the time and location of the exhibition. Ask students to invite parents, relatives, and other classes. Create posters or signs to advertise the exhibition.

5. Coach as needed. Encourage a variety of media, visual charts, etc.

6. Hold the exhibition.

7. Follow up with a discussion of the activity, what students learned, and what they would do the same or differently for future exhibitions.

Variations

1. Allow students to work in teams.

2. Visit a museum and arrange for the museum staff to explain its criteria for an exhibition.

3. Have students keep a journal of the steps taken in preparing the exhibition.

4. Brainstorm exhibition criteria with the students.

SCIENCE YEARBOOK

ACTIVITY-AT-A-GLANCE

Purpose

Create a visual and written record of class accomplishments in science.

When to Use

Use throughout the year as a synthesis of the year's science curriculum.

What You'll Need

❑ Duplication equipment and materials
❑ Camera

What to Do

1. At the start of the year, develop the criteria for a high-quality science yearbook. Post these in an area designated for yearbook-related information.

2. Create a yearbook staff for the science class. Be sure everyone has a job (e.g., photographers, writers, artists, editors) and knows his or her responsibilities.

3. Decide on the yearbook's format (e.g., sequential, thematic, etc.) and allow 1 day a month for students to work in class on their specific contributions.

4. Near the end of the year, spend 2 weeks in class assembling the yearbook. This is a key part of the year's review and a time to help students synthesize what they have learned.

IRI/SkyLight Training and Publishing, Inc.

190

5. Print or reproduce yearbooks and distribute at the end of the school year. Celebrate with a class dedicated to yearbook signing and reviewing students' accomplishments.

Variations

1. Allow students with like jobs to work as teams.
2. Keep a library of past yearbooks as models for the class.

BUBBLE TALK

ACTIVITY-AT-A-GLANCE

Purpose

Provide directions to a lab experiment.

When to Use

Use after teaching an important lab procedure to heighten students' recall and to increase their understanding of why the procedure is important.

What You'll Need

❏ Chart paper

What to Do

1. On the board or overhead, write a list of necessary steps to conduct a lab experiment. Form student pairs and assign each pair 1 step of the procedure.

2. Provide each pair with chart paper. Show students how to divide the paper into 4–6 sequenced boxes. In the boxes, the pair will illustrate 2 people performing a specific step of the procedure, using figures and bubbles to show dialogue and action.

3. After the "bubbles" are done, ask each pair to find other pairs who completed different steps of the procedure and to tape their drawings together in sequence to illustrate the entire procedure.

4. Display completed procedures and encourage students to view the completed projects. Close by mediating a discussion of this project's value.

Variations

1. Use bubbles to help students hypothesize about or imagine the thinking processes of famous scientists at work on a specific project (e.g., Thomas Edison, Marie Curie, Jonas Salk, Galileo).

2. Use bubbles to create cartoons that depict extreme positions on contemporary scientific issues.

3. Use illustrated procedures as instructions to perform an actual lab experiment.

DISCOVERY GAME

ACTIVITY-AT-A-GLANCE

Purpose

Use inductive reasoning skills to examine like items.

When to Use

Use as a lesson to introduce inductive reasoning or prior to a lesson introducing the use of microscopes to examine samples.

What You'll Need

❑ 7 canisters, water, mud, food dye, 5 different colors of gelatin

What to Do

1. Line up 7 similar canisters. In one, use a dye in water. In a second, put muddy water. Put a different color of solidified gelatin in each of the remaining canisters.

2. Draw a two-column T-chart on the board or overhead and label columns as "true" and "not true." Ask students to describe what they see. List student responses in the appropriate column of the chart.

3. After the lists are completed, ask students to explain why specific descriptions are in each column (i.e., the true statements are accurate observations or valid conclusions, the false statements are inaccurate observations or assumptions).

4. Explain that the type of thinking they used—arriving at a general conclusion from specific data—is called "inductive reasoning." Identify other instances where they have used or seen inductive

True	Not True
7 same-size canisters	2 canisters completely full
5 canisters with a solid of one color	1 canister with tea
2 canisters with liquid	
1 canister with blue water	
2 canisters 50% full	

reasoning (e.g., their parents deciding they are good or poor students based on report card grades).

Variations

1. Use pairs or trios. Give each group a set of samples that look alike in one way.
2. Use sample pieces of music that are alike in only one way.

FUTURISTIC SCIENCE FAIR

ACTIVITY-AT-A-GLANCE

Purpose

Design and build a prototype of a futuristic invention and display this invention at a futuristic science fair.

When to Use

Use as a motivating tool to stimulate creativity, hypothetical thinking, and interest in scientific concepts throughout the year.

What You'll Need

❑ Materials to build models
❑ Background information on futuristic displays at a world's fair

What to Do

1. Show pictures and tell a story about a world's fair that exhibited futuristic displays, or displays containing hypothetical future inventions. Identify some of the inventions that were displayed and whether they ever became real products.

2. Tell the class that it will end the school year by creating its own futuristic science fair. After each unit in science, brainstorm a list of ideas for futuristic inventions based on what students have learned. Post lists in a designated area.

3. Form mixed-ability invention teams. Each team will take 1 idea from the list and adapt and improve it, making the idea more useful and beneficial. Ask each student to draw a design of the future product.

4. Ask each team to review its members' designs and discuss the viability and feasibility of each in terms of building an actual model. Have students select 1 design and build a model of the new invention.

5. Have teams build displays to exhibit their models, create advertisements promoting their products, and write invitations to the fair to other classes, parents, and community members.

6. Set up and hold the fair.

Variations

1. Engage parents and community members to judge the fair. Give a variety of awards.

2. Have students build models and compete by demonstrating their inventions.

3. Create a class newsletter that includes news about the fair and drawings, articles, cartoons, surveys, and interviews about the inventions.

4. Draw parallels to manufacturers' design-to-production cycle (i.e., idea conception; design and revisions; analyses of materials, production method, labor costs; building prototypes; production; marketing and advertising). Ask each team to create a working portfolio that includes notes from brainstorming and planning sessions, all sketches, drawings, and doodles, and all other related materials. Upon completion of the project, ask each team to write a 5–6 paragraph essay describing its design-to-production process and to include examples from its portfolio to illustrate different stages of the process.

NATURE RUBBINGS

ACTIVITY-AT-A-GLANCE

Purpose

Demonstrate how symmetry appears in nature.

When to Use

Use at the beginning of a lesson or unit to introduce students to the concept of symmetry.

What You'll Need

❏ A variety of leaves
❏ Drawing paper and crayons

What to Do

1. Take the class on a nature walk. Have each student collect several leaves of different size, shape, and texture.

2. Ask students to cover each leaf, vein side up, with a sheet of paper and rub over it with a crayon.

3. Hang the completed rubbings and discuss the variations. Use different examples of rubbings to illustrate the symmetry in the leaves.

Variations

1. Select other plants to use for the rubbings. Contrast symmetry in tree leaves with other plant leaves.

2. Use clay to form impressions of leaves and/or plants. Have students soften the clay into patties that cover the leaves and stems so they can get a strong impression.

WINDOW TO THE WORLD

A MURAL

ACTIVITY-AT-A-GLANCE

Purpose

Collaborate on a class mural that illustrates concepts learned over an extended period.

When to Use

Use throughout the school year to motivate interest in science study and to help students communicate what they have learned through a visual medium.

What You'll Need

❑ Paint, brushes
❑ Wall, posterboards, or chart paper
❑ Pictures of sample murals

What to Do

1. Inform students at the beginning of the year or course that they will create a class mural at the end of the year/course that illustrates what they have learned. Show pictures of sample murals. Identify a place for the mural (e.g., a rotating wall in the cafeteria or hallway or even on a wall in the community).

2. During the year, brainstorm ideas for the mural after each unit, record ideas, and post in the room (or on a designated "Mural" bulletin board). Decide on a central unifying theme and tie ideas to this theme.

3. Begin to plan the mural a few months before the end of the year. Use a strategy that involves the entire class in the planning and painting of the mural. Review the criteria: the content of their science study must be central to what is depicted in the mural.

4. Paint the mural.

5. Use a rubric or other tool to assess both individual contributions and teamwork.

Variations

1. Divide the mural into sections and identify a class theme. Have students work in groups to complete designated sections of the mural.

2. If there is no wall available, use large strips of chart paper or posterboards taped together.

3. Create a Mural Graffiti board (using chart paper) where students post ideas and key concepts during a unit. Post new chart paper for each unit or whenever a sheet becomes full, save completed sheets, and use as a review of prior units during the actual planning stage of the mural.

SCIENTIFIC SCENARIO

ACTIVITY-AT-A-GLANCE

Purpose

Identify and research current issues and concerns presented in a case scenario.

When to Use

Use at the beginning of a lesson or unit to stimulate interest in a unit of study that has a connection to a current issue.

What You'll Need

❑ Copies of a scenario
❑ Access to library materials and/or the Internet

What to Do

1. Prepare a scenario related to the key concepts in a unit (e.g., deer eating local flora and fauna as an introduction to the food cycle). Be sure the scenario meets the following criteria:

   • Brief (2–3 paragraphs).

   • Describes a simple instance of a common problem.

   • Sets up a problem situation that is not easily solved.

   • Illustrates the issues central to the unit of study.

2. Distribute copies of the scenario to each student.

3. Assign students to find and read 2–3 articles related to the issue using library and/or Internet resources.

4. Conduct an all-class discussion, identifying the following:
   - The issue in the scenario.
   - How the specific case ties to a larger issue(s).
   - How the issue(s) relates to the unit of study.

Variations

1. Use several different scenarios on the same issue. Ask students to compare the key problem in each scenario to identify the main issue.
2. Use the Problem-Solving Model to identify the issue.
3. Assign students a 3–5 paragraph essay to report the results of their research. Request that they reference 1–2 facts or examples from the resource materials they used and identify sources in text. (Model a demonstration if introducing this concept or if students need a review.)

VIDEO RECORD

 ACTIVITY-AT-A-GLANCE

Purpose

Conduct an experiment that will be videotaped and use the videotape to identify individual performance, group technique, best practices, and areas for improvement.

When to Use

Use during a lesson to assess students' abilities, to identify "model" techniques for sharing with other students in the class, and to enable students to see themselves in action.

What You'll Need

❑ Video camera, VCR, and blank videotapes

What to Do

1. During a lab experiment, set up a video camera to tape 1 group. Instruct group members to narrate what they are doing as they perform the experiment.

2. View the videotape with the group upon completion of the experiment. Ask students to identify specific instances that illustrate strong techniques or model practices. Discuss the overall group technique and ways to improve it.

Variations

1. Record 1 group each day and view the tape with the group or entire class.

2. Edit a tape of best practices to share with the class.

3. Ask students to write individual assessments of both their own and the group's performance and to recommend 1 area for improvement.

JUST COLLECT IT

ACTIVITY-AT-A-GLANCE

Purpose

Learn the techniques of collecting and classifying animate and inanimate matter.

When to Use

Use throughout a lesson or unit to connect the learning of the process of classification to science units in the curriculum.

What You'll Need

❑ Posterboards and glue

What to Do

1. Activate students' prior knowledge of collecting. Ask students to share their collections of stamps, coins, or bottles or to bring in several examples.

2. Invite students to make a scientific collection to learn the principles of classification. As a class, select a curriculum-related object to collect. Conduct a collection hunt and help students gather many samples.

3. Ask students to sort the objects into at least 4 groups. Provide each student with a large sheet of posterboard and invite students to create visual displays of their collections that show this grouping. Have students label each group and note the "critical attribute" of each object that determined its inclusion in that group. Display the collections.

Variations

1. Take students on a field trip to a museum where they can see how collections are made on a grand scale.

2. Have students work in groups to collect items and construct visual displays.

3. Conclude by inviting parents to a museum night.

4. Invite students to collect and classify their favorite characters from literature.

AGREE/DISAGREE

ACTIVITY-AT-A-GLANCE

Purpose

Examine a position related to a scientific issue.

When to Use

Use this technique during a lesson or unit to wrap around a topical issue related to the curriculum.

What You'll Need

❏ Copies of Agree/Disagree Chart

What to Do

1. Introduce the class to a science-based current event issue in the community or state (e.g., laws regarding auto emissions, state wilderness preservation). Ask students to share what they know about the issue.

2. Distribute copies of the Agree/Disagree Chart. Using the board or overhead, list statements about the issue that show a variety of positions.

3. Allow time for students to check their position on each statement in the "Before" column.

4. Discuss areas where students agree and disagree. Probe and discuss reasoning on all positions. Collect charts for future use.

5. Study the topic and ask students to look for facts related to the agree/disagree statements.

 IRI/SkyLight Training and Publishing, Inc.

199

Agree/Disagree Chart

Topic: Overpopulation of deer

Statements	Before		After	
	Agree	Disagree	Agree	Disagree
1. Allow hunting to reduce number of deer.		X	X	
2. Deer hunting is cruelty to animals.	X			X
3. Deer are starving to death due to lack of vegetation.	X		X	
4. Deer are nuisances that destroy shrubbery and other plants.		X		X
5. Capture deer and relocate them in undeveloped areas.	X		X	

6. After studying the topic, redistribute the charts. Ask students to check the "After" column. Discuss changes in students' positions and probe for rationale behind their choices.

Variations

1. After students check their "before" positions, pair students with opposing views and hold an all-class debate.

2. Prior to studying the unit, pair students with opposing views. Ask students to write a persuasive letter to their partners in which they try to convince them to change their viewpoint. Upon completing the unit of study and reexamining their positions, ask students to respond to the original letters.

PROBLEM-SOLVING MODEL

ACTIVITY-AT-A-GLANCE

Purpose

Practice problem-solving skills, research a topic, and present information to the class.

When to Use

Use to develop students' problem-solving skills and provide practice in using content material to back up opinions and hypotheses.

What You'll Need

❑ No materials necessary

What to Do

1. Select a familiar topic from students' everyday lives and demonstrate a problem-solving process using the Problem-Solving Model.

    • Show the Problem-Solving Model.

    • Walk through the process by completing each column.

    • Review the steps in the model.

    • Bridge to a unit that lends itself to a problem-solving approach.

2. Demonstrate an example of using the model for a curriculum-related topic. Select a topic in the unit being studied that poses a "problem." As a class, brainstorm a list of how to fix or change the "problem"

The Problem	Strategies to Use	The Result
Garden plants are dying.	Water more often.	No change
	Inspect for bugs or diseases, and treat.	None observed
	Fertilize.	No change
	Thin seedlings.	Yes, spurt of growth after thinning

(e.g., how to prevent erosion, ending world hunger). List 3–4 examples in columns 2 and 3.

3. Form groups of 3–4 students. Select an all-class topic related to the unit and ask each group to use the problem-solving process to identify a recommended solution to the problem. Provide opportunities for the groups to meet as they study the unit to brainstorm possible solutions and record information on the Problem-Solving Model. Encourage students to gather information from the curriculum material and use it to solve the problem. Establish criteria for success: demonstrating key information, specificity of examples, and well thought out solutions.

4. At the end of the unit, ask each group to recommend 1 solution to the problem and prepare a presentation to the class explaining its choice and the rationale behind its decision. Conduct presentations. Use peer, teacher, and self-assessments. Close with a review of the model as it relates to the scientific method.

Variations

1. Use in conjunction with a unit or lesson on researching skills. Require students to use reference materials to obtain additional information on their topics and to use this information to support their recommended solutions.

2. In place of class presentations ask each group to write a letter to the editor explaining its solution and defending its position. Display letters on a large mock-up of a newspaper editorial page or compile all letters in a sample newspaper and distribute copies to students.

GLOSSARY

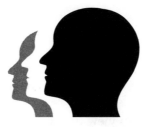

ABC criteria — Identification of goal as being achievable, believable, and controllable.

Aha — The moment of discovery when one learns something new or a confusing concept suddenly becomes clear; also called eureka.

Artifact — End product of student work, such as an essay, story, sketch, sculpture, mobile, writing sample, or artwork.

Attribute web — Visual diagram that illustrates attributes or characteristics of a topic or concept.

Base group — Core group of students who work together over an extended period.

Brainstorm — Group process to trigger spontaneous, fluent production of ideas.

Bridge — Connection or transition between concepts or units; often used to connect new information with familiar concepts or prior knowledge.

Carousel — Group rotation to view displayed student work at multiple locations throughout a room.

Concept map — Visual diagram that illustrates relationships in free flowing thoughts.

Cooperative group — Structured small group in which members have designated roles and responsibilities.

DOVE guidelines — Guidelines to promote an open, nonjudgmental environment for group sharing. DOVE is an acronym representing the following: Defer judgment; Opt for original ideas; Vast number is needed; Expand by piggybacking on others' ideas.

Fishbone — A diagram used to illustrate cause-effect relationships.

Four corners — Each corner of the room represents a different idea. Students are asked to select an idea and move to that corner for discussion.

Graphic organizer — Visual format used to organize ideas, concepts, and information. Also called visual organizer.

Human graph — Simulation of graph with participants physically positioning themselves along a continuum to indicate degree of agreement with an idea or issue.

Hurrah — Cheer and/or physical movement used to celebrate people and accomplishments (e.g., Whirley Bird, Standing "O"vation).

Jigsaw — Cooperative learning strategy that distributes portions of a whole to each person in a group to learn and then teach to the other members of the group.

Journal — A student diary consisting of verbal and visual entries that usually include personal reflections, self-assessments, and spontaneous writing.

KWL — Visual organizer to illustrate what one **k**nows about a topic, what one **w**ants to know, and what was **l**earned; oftentimes used to identify prior knowledge of a topic.

Likert scale — Measurement tool that assesses performance on a gradient scale. Also used to rate opinions, show a position on an issue, and indicate frequency of occurrence (e.g., 1 = never, 3 = sometimes, 5 = always).

Log — A student record consisting of verbal and visual entries reflecting personal reactions to learning, usually in relation to a specific course or topic.

Matrix — Chart that classifies items by dual categories—those given in both a column and a row. Items must meet the criteria of both categories.

Mind map — Visual representation of thinking strategy that starts with a central idea and branches off to new ideas; can include pictures, patterns, and colors.

Mrs. Potter's Questions — Mrs. Potter represents a teacher who asks students to use four questions to assess their learning and performance: What was I expected to do? What did I do well? If I did the same task again, what would I do differently? What help do I need?

Paired think-aloud — Strategy that involves one person in a pair verbalizing his or her thinking as the partner listens, monitors, and then asks questions for clarification.

PMI — Graphic organizer and/or thinking strategy used to identify the pluses, minuses, and interesting (or intriguing) questions related to an activity or lesson (developed by Edward de Bono, 1976).

Portfolio — Collection of student work, usually comprised of a student's best work or work that shows development. Also used to collect a group's or class's work.

Portmanteau — Strategy of combining two words to create another word with a new meaning (e.g., toehole—a hole in one's sock that expands as one plays with it).

Problem solving — Specific strategies that use creative synthesis and critical analysis to generate viable alternatives to perplexing situations.

Problem-solving model — Visual organizer used to identify a problem, list strategies to use to solve the problem, and describe results of each strategy.

Question web — Visual diagram showing questions and answers branching off a central concept or idea.

Random check — Assessment of student learning at sporadic moments or not based on a pattern or schedule.

Ranking — Rating system that prioritizes choices.

IRI/SkyLight Training and Publishing, Inc.

Rebus — Representation of words through pictures and symbols.

Round robin — Response in turn around a group.

Rubric — Assessment tool that specifies criteria for different levels of performance.

Self-assessment — Any tool or strategy used by an individual to examine and evaluate one's own work.

Sequence chart — Chart that lists steps of a process or procedure in the order in which they need to occur.

Six-inch voice — Soft voice that cannot be heard beyond a six-inch radius. Also called 10-centimeter voice.

Standard — Criterion used to assess performance.

Storyboard — A series of sketches that show action and dialogue.

T-chart — Chart made by writing a "t" to form two columns.

Target — Visual aid of three concentric circles used to identify priorities.

Think-pair-share — Strategy that allows individual thinking time, discussion with a partner, and then all-class sharing.

Three-story intellect verbs — Categorization of verbs to use in formulating questions that elicit responses based on different levels of thinking; e.g., one-story verbs prompt factual recall, two-story verbs ask for comparisons, reasoning, and generalizations, and three-story verbs stimulate imagination, hypotheses, and syntheses. Also called three-level questions.

Triple T-chart — T-chart with three columns.

Triple Venn diagram — Venn diagram comprised of three circles.

Venn diagram — Overlapping circles used to compare and contrast objects, people, ideas, etc.

Walk through — Demonstrate or model steps in a process or activity.

Web — Visual diagram that illustrates new ideas and concepts branching off of a central topic or idea.

Wraparound — A structured answering strategy in which students respond in turn.

IRI/SkyLight Training and Publishing, Inc.

Strategy Groupings

Assessment Tools

ABC criteria
Journal
Lead-in statement
Likert scale
Log
Mrs. Potter's Questions
Plus/Minus/Interesting (PMI)
Portfolio
Rating spectrum
Rubric
Scale
Standards
Targeted questions

Cognitive Strategies

Brainstorming
DOVE
Graphic organizer
Journal
Lead-in statement
Log
Think aloud

Cooperative Groupings

2-4-8
Base group
Carousel
Cooperative group
Expert jigsaw

Four corners
Heterogeneous group
Human graph
Interviewing
Jigsaw
Paired partners
People search
Round robin
Think-pair-share

Graphic Organizers

Agree/Disagree chart
Attribute web
Checklist
Concept map
Fishbone diagram
Four-column T-chart
KWL chart
Likert scale
Looks Like/Sounds Like T-Chart
Matrix
Mind map
Pie chart
Plus/Minus/Interesting (PMI)
Problem-solving model
Sequence chart
Snapshot sequence chart
Story tree
Storyboarding
T-chart

Target
The Newspaper Model
Three-Story Intellect Verbs diagram
Triple T-chart
Venn diagram

Standing "O"vation
Thumbs Up
Wave
Whirley Bird
Yes, Yes, Yes

Hurrahs/Energizers

Alaska Hurrah
Brain Wave
Double Clam Clap
Silent Cheer
Silent Clap

Reflective Strategies

Journal
Log
Mrs. Potter's Questions
PMI
Portfolio

BLACKLINES

Agree/Disagree Chart

Topic: _____

Statements	BEFORE		AFTER	
	Agree	Disagree	Agree	Disagree

IRI/SkyLight Training and Publishing, Inc.

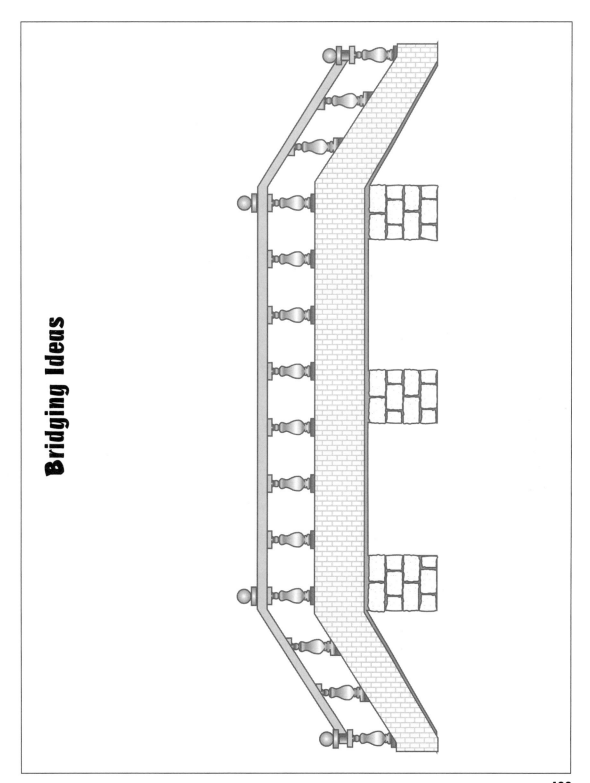

Bridging Ideas

Fishbone Diagram

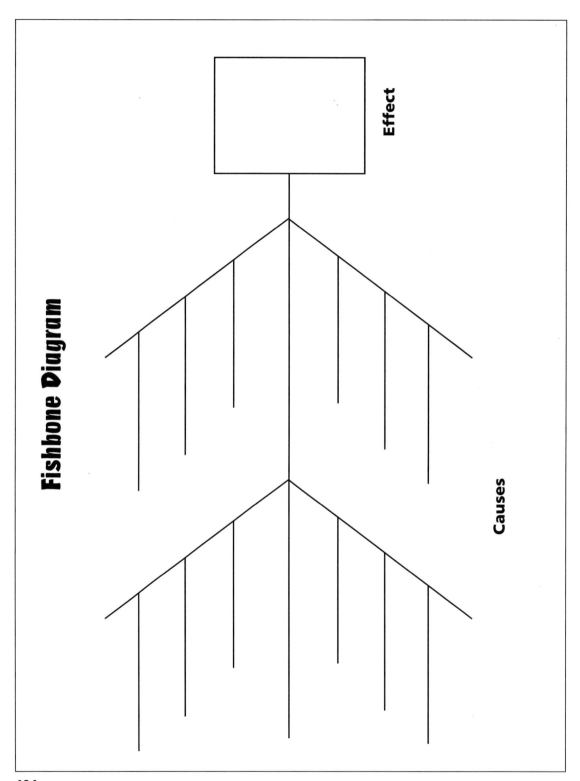

Effect

Causes

IRI/SkyLight Training and Publishing, Inc.

Goal Chart

Goal	Rank	Why Important	How to Achieve	Checkup	By When

Group Assessment

Group Name_____ **Date**_____

Activity_____

Members	Roles
_____	_____
_____	_____
_____	_____
_____	_____
_____	_____
_____	_____

What we did well

What we need to improve is

Questions we have

IRI/SkyLight Training and Publishing, Inc.

Hourglass

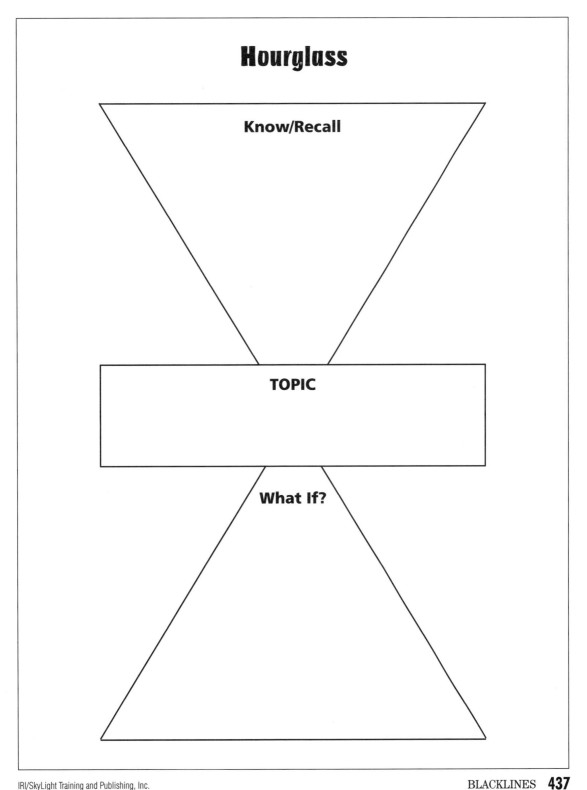

Know/Recall

TOPIC

What If?

Influence Chart

Important Person	How Related	Why Important	Influence	Results

IRI/SkyLight Training and Publishing, Inc.

Internet Hobby Search

1. What are your special interests?

2. What are your special talents?

3. What hobbies do you have that match your interests or talents?

4. What hobbies would you like to learn more about?

5. Pick one hobby and using the Internet identify resources for learning about this hobby.

Select 2–5 resources. Study them and prepare a 3–5 minute talk that describes the hobby, explains talents and/or skills needed for this hobby, and tells what your personal interest in this hobby is and how it might benefit you.

One-Minute Mirror

Goals

A Concern of the Day

A Success for Today

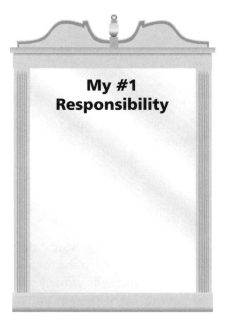

My #1 Responsibility

IRI/SkyLight Training and Publishing, Inc.

People Search

Find a Person Who . . .

1.

_____

2.

_____

3.

_____

4.

_____

5.

_____

6.

_____

7.

_____

8.

_____

Plus/Minus/Interesting (PMI)

P(+) Pluses	
M(–) Minuses	
I(?) Interesting Questions	

Problem-Solving Chart

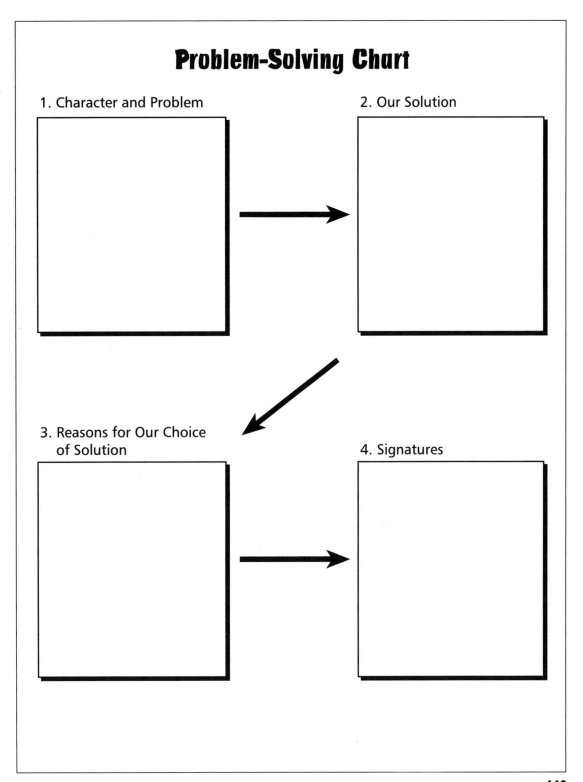

1. Character and Problem

2. Our Solution

3. Reasons for Our Choice of Solution

4. Signatures

Problem-Solving Model

The Problem	Strategies to Use	The Result

IRI/SkyLight Training and Publishing, Inc.

Scenarios

"Mary is a new girl in school. She has no friends. On the playground she is standing all by herself." Your group sees her. Decide how you can help her make friends. Make a play without words to show this.

"Juan has lost his milk for lunch." Decide what you can do to help him. Make a play without words to show this.

"Sue Ellen forgot to bring a note from home to go on the field trip." Decide what you can do to help her. Make a play without words to show this.

"Carl was in a fight on the bus with a bully. He is afraid to get on the bus again." Decide what you can do to help him. Make a play without words to show this.

"Marie was absent for a whole week. She has a lot of math to catch up." Decide what you can do to help her. Make a play without words to show this.

"Margaret's best friend was hurt. The friend fell from her bike and hit her head. The friend is in the hospital." Decide what you can do to help her. Make a play without words to show this.

"Carla's mom forgot to pick her up after school. Your sister is going to pick you and your friends up and drive you home." Decide how you can help her. Make a play without words to show this.

"Jamie lost his new team jacket. He thinks someone stole it." Decide how you can help him. Make a play without words to show this.

"Some big kids said mean things to Kate. They hurt her feelings." Decide how you can help her. Make a play without words to show this.

"Gerry just had a fight with her group. She walked away. She said she never wants to be in that group again." Decide how you can help her. Make a play without words to show this.

"Jo called Tony, her best friend, a bad name." Decide how you can help her make up to Tony. Make a play without words to show this.

"Tom doesn't have any lunch. He is very embarrassed." Decide how you can help him. Make a play without words to show this.

"A gang member wants Ralph to join the gang and deliver crack." Decide how you can help him say no. Make a play without words to show this.

Self-Progress Chart

Name_____

Check Date_____

Goal	Progress Check	End Date

IRI/SkyLight Training and Publishing, Inc.

Self-Review Questions

How far have I progressed toward my goals?

What are the barriers I have overcome?

What barriers yet remain?

What help do I need?

Sequence Chart

Topic:_____

IRI/SkyLight Training and Publishing, Inc.

Story Tree

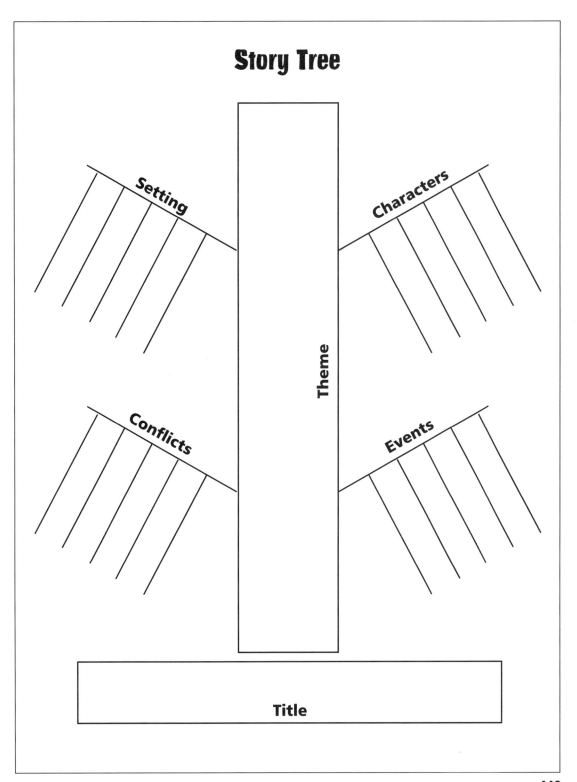

Setting

Characters

Theme

Conflicts

Events

Title

The Newspaper Model

Topic:

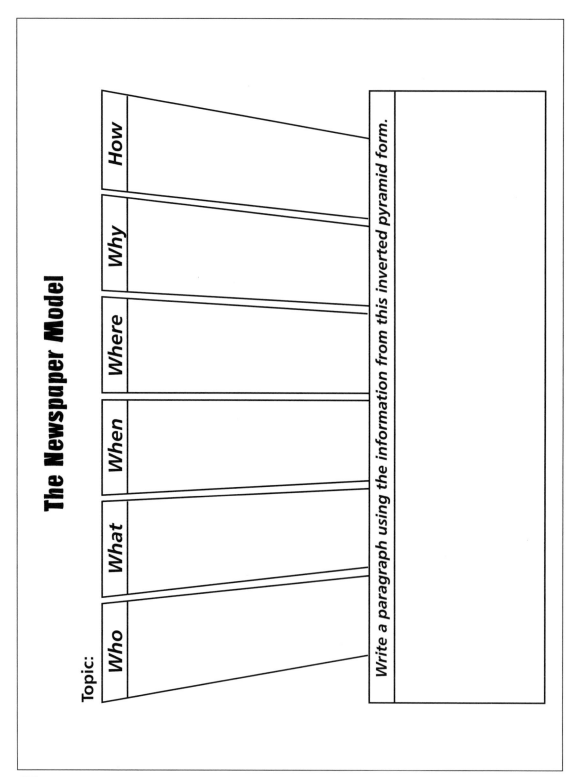

Who | What | When | Where | Why | How

Write a paragraph using the information from this inverted pyramid form.

Three-Story Intellect Verbs

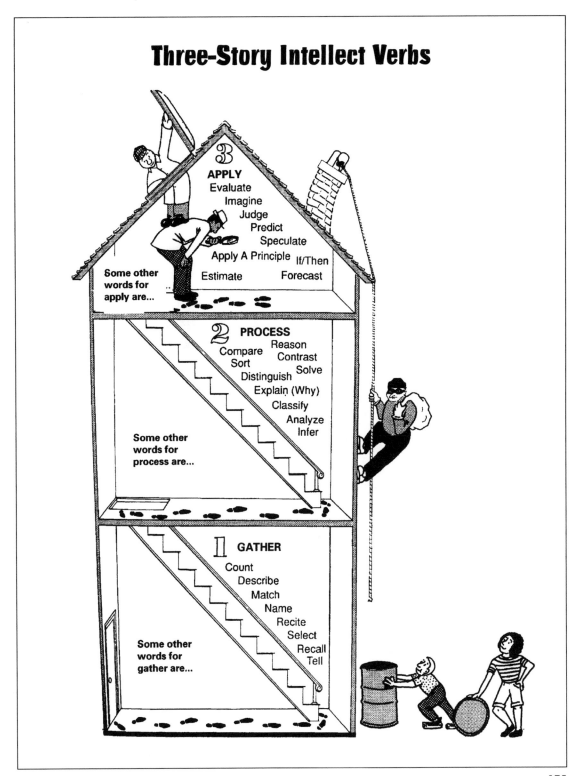

3 APPLY
Evaluate
Imagine
Judge
Predict
Speculate
Apply A Principle   If/Then
Estimate   Forecast

Some other
words for
apply are...

2 PROCESS
Reason
Compare   Contrast
Sort   Solve
Distinguish
Explain (Why)
Classify
Analyze
Infer

Some other
words for
process are...

1 GATHER
Count
Describe
Match
Name
Recite
Select
Recall
Tell

Some other
words for
gather are...

Triple Venn Diagram

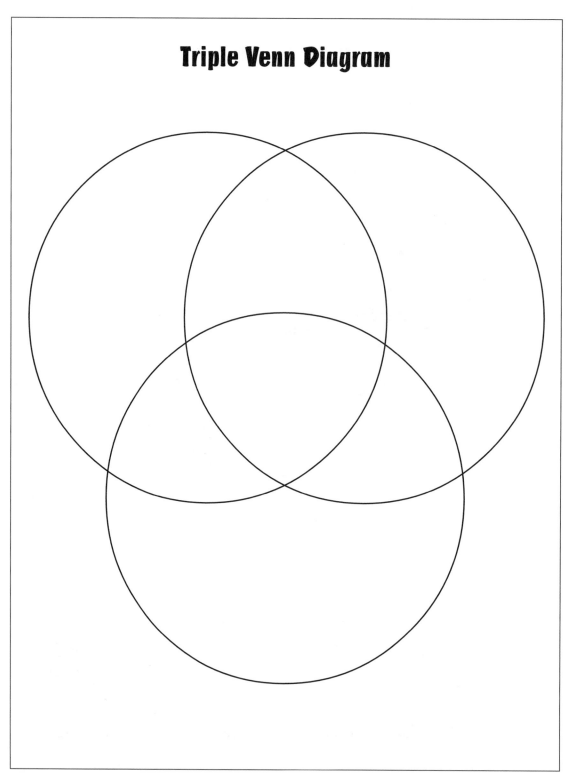

IRI/SkyLight Training and Publishing, Inc.

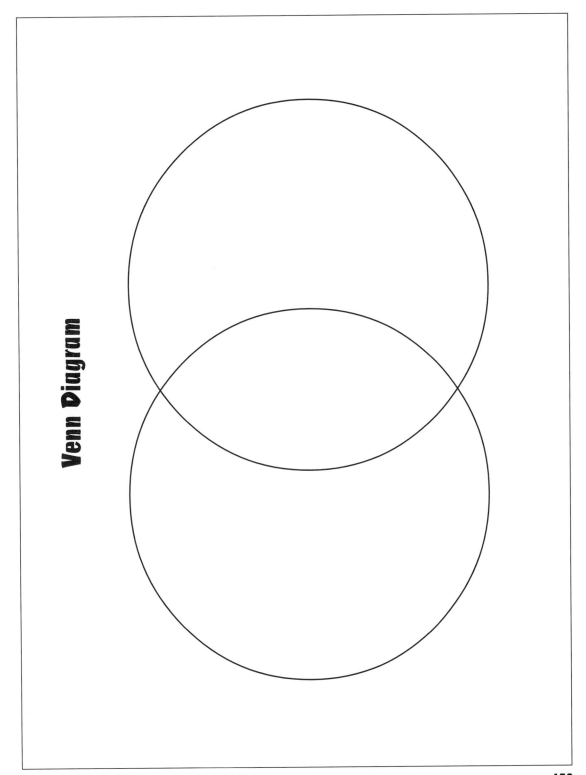

Venn Diagram

BIBLIOGRAPHY

Bellanca, James, and Robin Fogarty. *Blueprints for Thinking in the Cooperative Classroom.* Arlington Heights, IL: IRI/SkyLight Training and Publishing, 1991.

———. *Patterns for Thinking: Patterns for Transfer.* Arlington Heights, IL: IRI/SkyLight Training and Publishing, 1993.

Bellanca, James, and Robin Fogarty, editors. *Multiple Intelligences: A Collection.* Arlington Heights, IL: IRI/SkyLight Training and Publishing, 1995.

Bellanca, James, Carolyn Chapman, and Elizabeth Swartz. *Multiple Assessments for Multiple Intelligences (Course Edition).* Arlington Heights, IL: IRI/SkyLight Training and Publishing, 1997.

Berman, Sally. *A Multiple Intelligences Road to a Quality Classroom.* Arlington Heights, IL: IRI/SkyLight Training and Publishing, 1995.

Brown, Anne L., and Anne S. Palincsar. "Guided, Cooperative Learning and Individual Knowledge Acquisition." In *Knowing, Learning, and Instruction: Essays in Honor of Robert Glaser,* edited by L. B. Resnick. Hillsdale, NJ: Lawrence Erlbaum, 1989.

Campbell, Linda. *Teaching and Learning Through Multiple Intelligences.* Seattle, WA: New Horizons for Learning, 1992.

Chapman, Carolyn. *If the Shoe Fits . . . How to Develop Multiple Intelligences in the Classroom.* Arlington Heights, IL: IRI/SkyLight Training and Publishing, 1993.

Chapman, Carolyn, and Lynn Freeman. *Multiple Intelligences Centers and Projects.* Arlington Heights, IL: IRI/SkyLight Training and Publishing, 1996.

de Bono, Edward. *Teaching Thinking.* New York: Penguin, 1976.

Feuerstein, Reuven et al. *Instrumental Enrichment: An Intervention Program for Cognitive Modifiability.* Baltimore, MD: Univ. Park Press, 1980.

Fogarty, Robin. *Problem-Based Learning and Other Curriculum Models for the Multiple Intelligences Classroom.* Arlington Heights, IL: IRI/SkyLight Training and Publishing, 1997.

Fogarty, Robin, and Judy Stoehr. *Integrating Curricula with Multiple Intelligences: Teams, Themes, and Threads.* Arlington Heights, IL: IRI/ SkyLight Training and Publishing, 1995.

Gardner, Howard. *Frames of Mind: The Theory of Multiple Intelligences.* New York: Basic Books, 1983.

————. *Multiple Intelligences: The Theory in Practice.* New York: HarperCollins, 1993.

————. "Reflections on Multiple Intelligences: Myths and Messages." *Phi Delta Kappan* (November 1995).

Lazear, David. *Seven Ways of Knowing: Teaching for Multiple Intelligences.* 2d ed. Arlington Heights, IL: IRI/SkyLight Training and Publishing, 1991.

————. *Seven Ways of Teaching: The Artistry of Teaching with Multiple Intelligences.* Arlington Heights, IL: IRI/SkyLight Training and Publishing, 1991.

————. *Seven Pathways of Learning: Teaching Students and Parents About Multiple Intelligences.* Tucson, AZ: Zephyr, 1993

Martin, Hope. *Multiple Intelligences in the Mathematics Classroom.* Arlington Heights, IL: IRI/SkyLight Training and Publishing, 1996.

Murnane, Richard, and Frank Levy. *Teaching the New Basic Skills: Principles for Educating Children to Thrive in a Changing Economy.* New York: Free Press, 1996.

O'Connor, Anna T., and Sheila Callahan-Young. *Seven Windows to a Child's World: 100 Ideas for the Multiple Intelligences Classroom.* Arlington Heights, IL: IRI/SkyLight Training and Publishing, 1994.

Perkins, David, and G. Salomon. "Teaching for Transfer." *Educational Leadership.* 46 (September 1988): 22–23.

INDEX

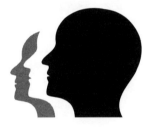

A

ABC criteria, 332–33, 336–37

Agree/disagree chart, 306–7, 418–19

Assessment tool, xxiv. *See also* Reflection.
    criteria, 42, 44–45, 314–15, 381, 398–99,
        400–1
    ABC, 332–33, 336–37
    group-assessment card, 312–13
    Likert scale, 244–45
    Mrs. Potter's questions, 313, 368–70
    observation checklist, 286–87, 288–89
    plus or minus, 358–59
    PMI (plus/minus/interesting) chart, 41,
        52–53, 230, 313, 330–31, 335, 364–65
    portfolio, 346–47, 379
    rating spectrum, 96–97
    rubric, 18–19, 58–59, 104–5, 158–59, 347
    scale, 158–59
    self-progress chart, 326–27
    self-review, 336–37
    song, 216–17
    standard, 310–11, 344–45
    videotape, 414–15

Attribute web, 238

Autobiography, 360–61

B

Base group. *See* Group.

Bodily/kinesthetic intelligence, xvii, xxv, xxvii,
    162–212

Body map, 210–12

Brown, Anne, xx, xxi

C

Cause and effect, 106–8, 396–97

Checklist, 31, 286–87, 288–89

Cheer, 190, 240–41, 276–77

Class logo, 274–75

Class magazine, 44–45

Class news station, 50–51

Class newsletter, 407

Class newspaper, 9, 389

Classifying, 80–81, 376–77

Coaching card, 90–91

Collage, 142–43, 264–65

Collecting, 80–81, 416–17

Concept map, 11, 13, 112–13, 117, 343

Cooperative group. *See* Group.

D

Dance, 178–79, 182–83

Decision making, 342–43, 362–63. *See also*
    Goal, Prioritizing, Problem solving.

Diagram. *See* Graphic organizer.

Dialogue balloon, 152–53, 156–57, 402–3

DOVE guidelines, 242, 318–19

E

Editorial, writing, 8–9, 26–27

Energizer, 186–87, 188, 190, 198–99, 206,
    240–41, 276–77

Exercise. *See* Physical exercise.

Expository writing. *See* Writing.

F

Feuerstein, Reuven, xx, xxi, xxv

Field trip, 230–31, 237, 417

Fishbone diagram, 106–8, 396–97

G

Game. *See also* Physical exercise.
    catch the dragon's tail, 202–3
    invent a sport, 204–5
    knots, 206
    mathematical skills, 92–93, 102–3
    playground races, 184–85

Garden, 372–73

Gardner, Howard, xv, xvi–xix, xxi, xxiv, xxv

Goal. *See also* Decision making, Problem
    solving.
    ABC criteria for, 332–33, 352–53
    charting, 326–27, 356–57
    group, 266–67, 270–71
    prioritizing, 322–23, 352–53
    reviewing, 158–59, 326–27, 332–33,
        334–35, 336–37, 358–59
    setting, 266–67, 270–71, 324–25, 332–33,
        348–49, 352–53, 356–57
    stretch, 166–67

Graphic organizer, xxiv
    agree/disagree chart, 306–7, 418–19
    chart, 204–5, 373

checklist, 31, 286–87, 288–89
concept map, 112–13, 117
fishbone diagram, 106–8, 396–97
goal chart, 356–57
hourglass graphic, 110–11
influence chart, 350–51
KWL chart, 114–15, 372
Likert scale, 244–45
map, 140–41, 394–95
matrix, 249, 278, 282–83, 284–85, 367,
    376–77, 411
newspaper model, 40–41
observation chart, 378–79
one-minute mirror, 324–25
plus or minus, 358–59
PMI (plus/minus/interesting) chart, 41,
    52–53, 230, 313, 330–31
problem-solving chart, 54–56
problem-solving model, 86–87, 88–89,
    338–40, 413, 420–22
problem-solving strategy wheel, 88–89
self-progress chart, 326–27
sequence chart, 64–65, 94–95, 150–51,
    360–61, 402–3
story tree, 42–43
storyboard, 148–49
T-chart, 18–19, 52–53, 164–65, 200–1,
    273, 290–91, 301, 343, 358–59, 370
target, 322–23
three-legged stool, 36–37
three-story intellect verbs diagram, 46–48,
    280–81
timeline, 10, 348–49, 360–61
Venn diagram, 98–99, 138–39, 230,
    232–33, 278, 386–87
web, 14–15, 116–17, 196–97, 200–1, 238,
    282–83
Graph, 70–71, 76–77, 85, 130–31, 194–95
Group
    2-4-8, 306–7
    ad, 278–79
    assessment card, 312–13
    base, 294–95, 296–97, 364–65
    bonding, 238–39, 264–65, 270–71,
        274–75, 276–77, 278–79, 296–97,
        300–1, 304–5, 306–7

cheer/song, 238–39, 240–41, 276–77
collage, 264–65
cooperative, xxiv, xxvi, 260, 266–67,
    270–71, 272–73, 280–81, 288–89, 292–
    93, 300–1, 302–3, 396–97, 420–22
heterogeneous, 266–67, 268–69, 294–95,
    302–3, 420–22
logo, 274–75
mobile, 300–1
motto, 288–89, 304–5
name, 296–97

H

Haiku, 254–55
Heterogeneous group. *See* Group.
Hourglass graphic, 110–11
Hurrah, 198–99

I

Icebreaker, 60–61, 348–49
Influence chart, 350–51
Internship, 392–93
Interpersonal intelligence, xviii, xx, xxiv, xxv,
    xxvii, 264–315
Interviewing, 46–48, 382–83, 392–93
Intrapersonal intelligence, xviii, xx, xxiv, xxv,
    318–70

J

Jigsaw, 62–63, 282–83, 284–85, 329
Journal, xxiv, 2–3, 4–6, 20–21, 52–53, 159,
    167, 201, 231, 305, 320–21, 327, 337,
    347, 349, 352, 358–59, 375, 392–93,
    399. *See also* Log.
    gardening, 373
    vocabulary, 2–3

K

Kinesthetic intelligence. *See* Bodily/kinesthetic
    intelligence.
KWL chart, 114–15, 372

L

Lab experiment
    videotaping, 414–15
    writing directions for, 402–3

Timeline, 10, 348–49, 360–61
Transfer, xxii

V

Venn diagram, 98–99, 138–39, 230, 232–33, 278, 386–87
Verbal/linguistic intelligence, xv, xvi, xxv, xxvii, 1–56
Videotaping, 50–51, 393, 414–15
Visual/spatial intelligence, xv, xvi, xxiv, xxv, xxvii, 110–59
Visual organizer. *See* Graphic organizer.
Vocabulary, 2–3, 28–29, 136–37

W

Web/webbing, 14–15, 116–17, 196–97, 200–1, 236–37, 282–83, 284–85. *See also* Map/mapping.
Writing. *See also* Journal, Lead-in statement, Letter, Log.

autobiography, 360–61
cheer, 240–41
class newsletter, 407
directions for lab experiment, 402–3
editorial, 8–9, 26–27
essay, 36–37, 388–89, 413
expository, 34–35, 36–37, 38–39, 40–41
haiku, 254–55
narrative, 34–35, 38–39, 50–51
news story, 50–51
newspaper model for, 40–41
persuasive, 38–39, 50–51, 364–65
poem, 250–51, 252–53, 254–55, 256–57
song, 214–15, 216–17, 220–21, 246–47, 276–77
sonnet, 256–57

Y

Yearbook, 400–1

Training and Publishing Inc.

We Prepare Your Teachers Today
for the Classrooms of Tomorrow

Learn from Our Books and from Our Authors!

Ignite Learning in Your School or District.

SkyLight's team of classroom-experienced consultants can help you foster systemic change for increased student achievement.

Professional development is a process, not an event. SkyLight's seasoned practitioners drive the creation of our on-site professional development programs, graduate courses, research-based publications, interactive video courses, teacher-friendly training materials, and online resources—call SkyLight Training and Publishing Inc. today.

SkyLight specializes in three professional development areas.

Specialty #

Best Practices

We **model** the best practices that result in improved student performance and guided applications.

Specialty #

Making the Innovations Last

We help set up **support** systems that make innovations part of everyday practice in the long-term systemic improvement of your school or district.

Specialty #

How to Assess the Results

We prepare your school leaders to encourage and **assess** teacher growth, **measure** student achievement, and **evaluate** program success.

Contact the SkyLight team and begin a process toward long-term results.

Training and Publishing Inc.

2626 S. Clearbrook Dr., Arlington Heights, IL 60005
800-348-4474 • 847-290-6600 • FAX 847-290-6609

There are
one-story intellects,
two-story intellects, and three-story
intellects with skylights. All fact collectors, who
have no aim beyond their facts, are one-story men. Two-story men
compare, reason, generalize, using the labors of the fact collectors as
well as their own. Three-story men idealize, imagine,
predict—their best illumination comes from
above, through the skylight.

—*Oliver Wendell*
Holmes

Training and Publishing Inc.